Praise

'The definitive book for furniture retail, one the whole trade should be grateful for. From the shop floor to the boardroom, it sets out service-led sales principles that transform performance, raise standards and restore pride in the profession. The practical, deeply human approach that defines Adam and the FSS workshops runs through every page.'

— **Nathan Doe**, Managing Director of John Doe of Diss

'*Selling Furniture* distils decades of frontline retail experience into a disciplined, structured framework written specifically for the furniture sector. Grounded in real stores and commercial reality, it turns behavioural insight into practical methods that can be applied immediately. In a market where marginal gains in conversion materially affect profitability, this is more than a sales manual – it has the depth, clarity and sector relevance to become a defining reference point for furniture retailers committed to raising standards and delivering measurable results.'

— **Paul Farley**, Editor-in-Chief, Furniture News

'Having known and worked with Adam for over thirty years, his results speak for themselves. This book gives you the "how". Correctly implemented, it's worth millions.'

— **Gary Pitchford**, International Furniture Buyer, GSP

'The book is a testament to Adam Hankinson's commitment, service excellence and copious experience. It is the Holy Bible of Furniture Sales. The book will not only help shape you in the workplace, but in your daily life. How to combat adversities, how to accept reward and, most importantly, how to consistently be the best YOU. The guidance will ensure the mechanics of the Seven Habits are on standby mode in the mind's eye before naturally navigating through the processes to get the best out of ANY situation, wherever and whoever you are! The possibilities are endless and the potential uncapped! A masterpiece!'

— **Luke Gilby**, General Manager, Bradbeers Furniture

'This book is as powerful as Adam's live training – practical, relatable and immediately usable. So, are you ready to raise your standards, because everything you need is in this book?'

— **Ryan Pheloung**, Owner Bradfords New Zealand

'This book is a masterpiece of timeless sales expertise that made me think about my team, specific areas to work on and areas to immediately improve on – absolute gold!'

— **Jamie Wetton**, Branch Manager, Nick Scali

'No gimmicks. No waffle. Just the stuff that works: ask better questions, listen harder than your competitors, link everything back to what they told you and earn the right to close. That's why this book prints money.'

— **Paul Atherton**, The Virtual Sales Director and creator of NeuroClose™

'*Selling Furniture* by Adam Hankinson is an outstanding guide for anyone serious about excelling in furniture retail. Drawing on over forty-five years of hands-on industry experience, Adam delivers a practical, no-nonsense framework built around seven powerful habits – mindset, approach, foundation questions, listening, selling the solution, concluding and referrals and recommendations. Each habit is grounded in the real-world challenges of today's showroom floor and is packed with actionable tips, tools and techniques that can be implemented immediately and referred to for years to come. We've been fortunate enough to apply, test and refine these seven habits in our own sales process, and the results have been undeniable – more confidence, stronger customer relationships and, most importantly, a genuine increase in sales.'

— **David Philp**, Director, Gillies of Broughty Ferry

No gimmicks. No waffle. Just the stuff that works: ask better questions, listen harder than your competitors, link everything back to what they told you and earn the right to close. That's why this book earns its money.'

— Paul Atherton, The Virtual Sales Director and creator of NeuroClose™

'*Selling Furniture* by Adam Hartford is an outstanding guide for anyone serious about excelling in furniture retail. Drawing on over forty-five years of hands-on industry experience, Adam delivers a practical, no-nonsense framework built around seven powerful habits: mindset, approach, foundation questions, listening, selling the solution, concluding and referrals and recommendations. Each habit is grounded in the real-world challenges of today's showroom floor and is packed with actionable tips, tools and techniques that can be implemented immediately and returned to for years to come. We've been fortunate enough to apply, test and refine these seven habits in our own sales process, and the results have been undeniable – more confidence, stronger customer relationships and, most importantly, a genuine increase in sales.'

— David Philp, Director, Gillies of Broughty Ferry

SELLING FURNITURE

THE MILLION-POUND SELLER BLUEPRINT

The Seven Habits of the Most Effective Furniture Salespeople

ADAM HANKINSON

Rethink

First published in Great Britain in 2026
by Rethink Press (www.rethinkpress.com)

Contents

Foreword

For most customers, buying furniture is the third largest purchase they will ever make – after their home and their car. It is a considered decision, combining emotional importance with long-term financial value. That makes it vital they feel confident not just in what they buy, but in who they buy it from. Trust, reassurance and professionalism are not optional in furniture retail – they are fundamental.

Real success in this industry is therefore rarely accidental. It is built quietly, habit by habit, conversation by conversation over time. The most effective salespeople do not rely on charisma or chance – they rely on standards, consistency and a deep respect for both the customer and the craft.

Housing Units is a long-established, high-quality home furnishings retailer operating at the premium end of the market. Founded in 1947, we are proud to be approaching our eightieth year and to stand as one of the largest independent furniture stores in the United Kingdom, serving customers from across the North and far beyond. Our reputation has been built carefully over eight decades and is something we protect fiercely. Any approach to sales training or development must honour that history, reflect our values and enhance, never compromise, the experience our customers expect from us.

It was with that perspective that we began working with Adam Hankinson and his team. Like many retailers of our scale, we approached the decision with a degree of trepidation. We had invested in people development before and had experience of different trainers, frameworks and methodologies, some more successful than others. We had also heard positive feedback from other respected businesses within the industry, but reputation alone is never enough. The real test is whether something genuinely works in your own environment, with your own people.

That question becomes even more important when working with experienced sales teams. Credibility matters. If salespeople sense that a trainer does not truly understand the realities of furniture retail, engagement is lost very quickly. What became clear early on is that Adam and his team bring depth of experience that is immediately recognisable on the shop floor. Their knowledge is specific, practical and grounded in furniture retail. Because of that, even our most experienced people bought into the process and found that there were still techniques, habits and refinements that could make a meaningful difference.

From the outset, it was also clear that this approach was not about scripts, pressure or forcing behaviour that feels unnatural. That was essential for us. Our business is built on long-term relationships, trust and professionalism. Any development programme has to reinforce those principles, not undermine them. This work respects individuality while raising standards, helping people sell with confidence, structure and consistency – without ever becoming robotic.

The programme demands discipline, consistency and application. It rewards those who commit to it properly and understand that progress is built through focus and repetition. That commitment has to come from both sides. When the business is as invested in making it work as Adam and his team are in delivering it, the results follow.

Adam's passion and enthusiasm for furniture sales is unmistakable. It runs through his work, his coaching and his standards. He understands that selling at a high level is not about pressure or performance, but about doing the right things, in the right order, often enough that they become instinctive – and this book captures that approach with clarity and conviction.

As a furniture business owner, I have seen first-hand how small improvements gather momentum. A stronger approach at the door. Better questions. More deliberate listening. A clearer conclusion. Individually, these changes may seem modest, but together they transform confidence, consistency and results. They are especially valuable at times when footfall is more challenging. When opportunities are harder won, being more effective with the customers who do come through the door becomes critical.

Over the years, I've had the privilege of visiting some of the most impressive furniture stores around the world. Incredible buildings, beautifully designed showrooms, world-class product and significant investment in the environment. Yet too often there is a gap between the owner's vision for excellence and the experience being delivered on the sales floor.

When that gap exists, something important is lost: the opportunity to build trust, to guide customers with confidence and to fully justify the value of what's on display. A great store should elevate the experience, not expose inconsistencies between the surroundings and the conversation. Without consistent, confident and professional selling, even the most impressive showroom cannot fully deliver on its promise.

You can have outstanding product, an inspiring retail environment and a sales experience to match. This is where the principles in this book matter. The Seven

Habits provide the link between vision and execution, ensuring that the quality of the sales conversation matches the quality of the store itself.

What stands out about this book is how deliberately simple it is. It encourages discipline, reflection and ownership, recognising that lasting progress is built through focus, repetition and a process you can rely on.

Its relevance spans every level of a furniture business. For salespeople, it sharpens everyday conversations. For managers, it provides a practical coaching framework that drives consistency without micromanagement. For owners and directors, it offers reassurance – a clear line of sight between habits, culture and sustained commercial performance.

In a challenging and highly competitive market, our business has continued to improve sales performance at a time when many retailers are under pressure. That does not happen by accident. It is the result of skills being applied consistently, supported properly and embedded into day-to-day behaviour.

Adam and his team are not viewed as outsiders. They are trusted partners. People look forward to them being in the business, and over time they have come to feel like part of the wider team. That level of engagement speaks volumes.

This book is a clear, disciplined blueprint for turning great stores into great selling environments.

Stuart Fox, Managing Director, Housing Units (Manchester, UK)

Preface

In furniture stores everywhere, sales are lost every day.

Customers browse. Conversations don't quite start, don't quite progress and orders are not closed. Confidence wavers. Interest is not converted into commitment. Orders that could be taken are left open, delayed or lost altogether – not because people don't care, but because the right attitudes, skills and behaviours aren't always applied at the moments that matter most.

The reality is that fewer than 5% of furniture sales teams have ever received professional training in how to sell. Most people learn by observation, instinct and trial and error – doing their best without a clear blueprint.

The cost of that gap is significant.

In a typical UK furniture store, with an average order value of £2,000 and a team of six salespeople, just one missed order per person, per week equates to over £600,000 a year in lost revenue.

Selling Furniture exists to close that gap.

Built on over 100 years of combined experience and drawn directly from multi-award-winning sales transformation programmes used by many of the UK and Ireland's most progressive furniture retailers, this book brings together hundreds of practical tips, tools and techniques.

None of it is theory. Every idea, habit, question and technique has been tried, tested, refined and proven on real shop floors – taken directly from the very best salespeople, managers, coaches and trainers in the industry.

This is the Million-Pound Seller Blueprint.

The practical working bible of furniture retail sales.

Never before have so many proven, immediately applicable skills been brought together in one place. Applied consistently, they don't just improve performance – they compound it, week after week.

For salespeople, this book provides confidence, clarity and a clear path toward becoming a million-pound seller.

For managers, it offers a shared language and practical framework to develop more of their team to that level.

For owners and directors, it delivers a proven way to protect their investment, maximise marketing spend and ensure opportunities are converted, not wasted.

That's why this book really is worth millions.

Introduction: How High Performers Build The Right Habits

This book grew out of more than forty-five years in the furnishings industry – years spent travelling the country, listening to, coaching and supporting salespeople. Over two decades of that time were spent visiting stores week after week, meeting sales teams in every town and showroom you can imagine.

A foundation for the Seven Habits of the most effective furnishings salespeople

They weren't just the top billers, but committed, seasoned professionals with genuine strengths across different parts of the sales process. Some were exceptional at asking questions, others brilliant at building relationships, and many were natural closers. Each was successful in their own way.

A quote that is often attributed to the Greek philosopher Aristotle goes, 'We are what we repeatedly do. Excellence, then, is not an act but a habit.' When I asked, 'How do you do it?' the answers were often, 'I just do what I do,' or, 'People buy from people.' True, but that wasn't the full story. When we look closer, we start to see patterns. From one end of the country to the other, people who had never met each other were doing the same types of things – and they were consistently the *right things*. The details might vary, but the principles were strikingly similar. The common thread? Habits – often *unconscious* ones.

A habit is a behaviour repeated so often it becomes automatic – your brain's way of saving energy by cutting back on thinking time (*automaticity*). Every habit follows the same loop:

Cue → Craving → Response → Reward.

Here's how that looks in a sales environment:

A customer walks in (cue). Your brain predicts a reward – connection, conversation, perhaps a sale (craving). You smile and say, 'Good morning, how are you today?' (response). The customer replies warmly, you engage, and feel that lift of connection (reward). Repeat this often enough and it becomes instinctive – that's how excellence turns into habit. As James Clear says in his book *Atomic Habits,* 'You do not rise to the level of your goals. You fall to the level of your systems.'[1]

You've probably heard that it takes twenty-one days to form a new habit. That idea actually came from a book written in the 1960s by a plastic surgeon who noticed that his patients took about three weeks to adjust to their new appearance. It was never intended as a rule for behaviour change – but it stuck.

Later, research from University College London found that forming a new habit – such as drinking more water or exercising daily – takes, on average, sixty-six days. However, that's just an average. In reality, the range was between eighteen and 254 days, depending on how complex the behaviour was and how often it was repeated. The key insight? It isn't really the number of *days* that matters – it's the number of *repetitions.*

Each time you repeat a behaviour, the brain strengthens the neural connection that links cue, response and reward.

Think about learning to tie your shoelaces as a child. If you only practised once a day, it might have taken months before you could do it without thinking. However, if someone had made you practise for two hours straight – keeping it fun, challenging, even rewarding – you'd have mastered it much faster.

Habits work the same way. The more frequently and deliberately you repeat the right action, the faster your brain locks it in. *Repetition is the mother of skill* – the more often you practise a behaviour the right way, the faster it will become automatic.

Real change is a process, not a sprint. However, once habits form, they compound like interest: small daily wins that build unstoppable momentum. Every time you reinforce a new habit – even a small one – you teach your brain, *this is who I am now.*

A customer walks in and you say, 'You OK there? Give us a shout if you need any help.' That's a habit, just not a helpful one. It feels safe, but it shuts down conversation.

Replacing it with, 'Good morning, how are you today?' (pause for a genuine answer), then 'What brings you in?' feels less comfortable at first – and that's exactly where growth lives. This new version takes awareness and a small leap out of your comfort zone. Repeat it enough times and it stops feeling awkward; it becomes your new normal.

Here's the point: we all carry *unconscious competencies* and *unconscious incompetencies*. This book explores both. It shines a light on what already works (so you can do more of it) and exposes the reflexes that hold you back (so you can replace them).

Together, we'll explore the nuances of sales – the small, repeatable activities and behaviours that shift sales outcomes – and we'll create a clear roadmap for improving your sales skill set across hundreds of tiny moments in your interactions with customers.

High performers practise the right things until they become second nature. They step beyond their comfort zone daily, until a higher standard becomes their new normal. James Clear's *Atomic Habits* nails it again when he said, 'Every action you take is a vote for the type of person you wish to become.'[2]

The Seven Habits that are explored in this book are already alive in the best salespeople, and we all have the ability to use them more often to improve our conversations with customers. The key is to focus, and to identify and name them. Once you see them clearly, you can practise them deliberately – and small improvements will quickly gather pace.

What's in it for me?

Before we go further, it's worth asking yourself a simple question: what's in this for me?

If you're a salesperson, using the Seven Habits will equip you with a stronger, more reliable skillset on the shop floor. You'll become more consistent from one customer to the next, more assured in your conversations and more effective at turning interest into commitment. This means more control over your results and, ultimately, more commission in your pocket. Beyond the money, that control removes the need to rely on luck or mood. You'll know what to do, when to do it and why it works. Master the Seven Habits and you'll give yourself a better chance to become a million-pound seller. If you're a manager, these habits provide consistency of attitudes and behaviours, quality of conversation with every customer and professionalism in every interaction. This will then deliver consistent results.

If you're an owner or director, the value is strategic. These habits protect your marketing spend by making sure browsers are converted into buyers. They provide consistency across your teams, so you'll no longer have to worry about which staff member a customer happens to meet. And the return on investment is clear, one extra order per salesperson per week will transform your bottom line.

How to get the best from this book

As a specialist furniture sales training and development business, Furniture Sales Solutions (FSS), we ask people before every sales training workshop to write down the one thing they most want to gain from the experience. When you're using this book, the same principle applies, but the key is to be specific.

Don't try to change everything at once. Choose one or two habits or techniques that matter most to you right now, either as an individual, a manager or a business. Habits take time to build, and the real progress comes from focus and repetition.

Over time, these small, specific improvements create momentum and confidence. For a single salesperson, the reward could be one extra order a week. For a team of ten, that could mean hundreds of thousands of pounds in extra revenue every year. But beyond the numbers, the real value is confidence; confidence in yourself, in your process and in your ability to guide customers from browsing to buying.

There are certain critical concepts that you'll need to understand if you're to master the Seven Habits. These will be highlighted throughout the book.

As you go through this book, we suggest:

- You read it with a pen in hand, underlining, circling and making notes.
- You reflect on your own conversations as you go. Where do you recognise yourself? Where do you want to grow?
- You don't just read, you practise. Try the examples, roleplays and challenges with real customers. This is the most important point. Knowledge without action is just theory.

Action, applied consistently, is what turns the Seven Habits explored in this book into sales, confidence and long-term success.

Remember, everyone will use this book slightly differently:

- For the sales professional, it's a daily guide to sharpen skills, build confidence and continually improve.
- For the manager interested in the performance of their team, it's a coaching framework to raise standards, spot progress and grow consistency across each of its members.
- For the people- and results-oriented owner or director, it's a strategic tool, a way to protect marketing investment, strengthen culture and turn browsers into loyal customers.

However you use it, the goal is the same: small, deliberate improvements that compound into extraordinary results.

CASE STUDY: Housing Units, Hollinwood (Oldham)

Established in 1947, Housing Units has grown from a local builders' merchants in Hollinwood, Oldham, into one of the UK's most admired high-end home furnishings destinations. For more than seventy years, the business has built its reputation on exceptional service, attention to detail and a deeply personal shopping experience, the kind of environment where 'hard selling' would never belong.

When the team partnered with Furniture Sales Solutions, the goal was simple: to elevate performance without compromising that customer-first ethos. The training proved to be a perfect fit. Every habit and technique was rooted in understanding, empathy and confidence, helping colleagues to have clearer, more natural conversations that guided customers to the right decisions. The result was not a pushier experience, but a better one: higher conversions, greater consistency and a renewed sense of pride across the sales floor.

'We're a service-led, high-end department store, so anything that feels salesy is a nonstarter,' says Stewart Smith, Retail & Operations Director. 'The FSS approach is the opposite, customer focused, brand-safe and completely aligned with how we want our people to sell. It didn't make us more salesy; it made us more ourselves.'

1
The Mechanics Of Selling

'You can't teach people how to sell!' The sales director folded his arms, convinced he'd just closed the discussion. For him, selling was a gift, a kind of natural-born talent that some people possessed and others didn't.

Of course, there's some truth in that. Personality, charisma, charm and experience all play a part. They give salespeople their individuality, the unique style that makes them stand out and be memorable. However, here's the key: even the most talented salesperson in the world still needs a structure and probably has one without realising it.

That's because selling doesn't just come down to talent, it's a set of skills. Much of what selling comes down to is mechanical, repeatable behaviours – like how you approach, the questions you ask, how you listen, how you present and how you close. These are mechanics that can be learned, coached and improved.

A natural ability might give someone a head start, but long-term success comes from having a structure, a process to follow. The best salespeople in the world, whether they realise it or not, are applying mechanics, habits and actions in every conversation, which guide the customer through a proven journey.

That's what the mechanics of selling provide: the framework. The Seven Habits in this book are not a theory we've made up; they are distilled from the very best salespeople we've ever worked with. Different personalities, different backgrounds, different styles, but the same core process, coupled with discipline.

So yes, selling is more than mechanics. But without mechanics, you don't have selling, you just have conversation. This book is designed to show you those mechanics: the Seven Habits that make up the framework of world-class selling. Once you trust the process, the outcome takes care of itself.

The machine analogy

Think of selling as being like a well-run production line. In a factory, every stage matters. The right ingredients go in, each step is done in order, and what comes out at the end is a consistent, reliable product. Skip a stage or do things out of sequence, and the result is flawed.

Selling works the same way. A warm welcome sets the tone. Asking questions and listening reveal the customer's needs. Presenting the right solution makes the conversation relevant. Concluding with confidence secures the order. Miss one of those steps and, just like in the factory, the desired end product is not delivered.

Following a process doesn't mean being robotic. There is plenty of room for personality, empathy and flair to be layered on top, which bring the conversations to life. Customers don't feel like they're on a conveyor belt. Instead, they feel understood and guided by someone confident, professional and in control.

To see this in action, think about three simple but costly mistakes.

A customer walks into your store, wanders around for ten minutes, tries a sofa, glances at the price tag, and leaves. No one ever spoke to them. That was a sale that could have been yours.

Another customer is handed a brochure before a single question is asked. Instead of starting up a conversation, it ends up being a ticket out of the store. You've lost the chance to discover their needs and maybe lost them altogether.

Or, after a great conversation and strong rapport, a salesperson thanks the customer and lets them leave without asking for the order. All that value, all that effort, left on the table.

These moments may seem small, but when repeated over a week, a month or a year, they add up to thousands of pounds in lost revenue.

What am I best at?

When FSS run training workshops, this is often one of the first exercises we do. We ask people to think about their selling skills and name the things within a sales conversation they believe they do best. To help, we throw out examples: maybe they're strong on product knowledge, maybe they're confident at closing, maybe they're good at greeting and building rapport, maybe they're skilled at uncovering the customers' needs or handling their objections. What's striking is how often people pause and realise they've never really thought about it in this way before.

For many salespeople, this is the first time they pause and ask themselves what they are actually best at in a sales conversation. Until now, selling may have been largely instinctive. By consciously thinking about the conversation and recognising that a successful sale is made up of clear component parts, you can start to identify your natural strengths, understand what good really looks like at each stage, and then deliberately sharpen the areas that quietly limit your results. Take a moment to give yourself credit. It's not in most salespeople's nature to pat themselves on the back, but this reflection is how you begin your journey of awareness and realisation. I'll introduce the Seven Habits properly in a moment, but for now, try scoring yourself on a scale of 1 to 10, with 1 being 'terrible' and 10 being 'fantastic' on each of the below to uncover what your strengths and weaknesses are:

- **Mindset:** keeping a positive, focused attitude all day
- **Approach:** making customers feel at ease right from the start
- **Questions:** showing genuine curiosity and interest
- **Listening:** understanding what customers really mean
- **Selling the solution:** linking what you show to what matters to them
- **Conclude:** naturally guiding towards a confident close
- **Referrals and recommendations:** delighting people so they recommend you

Recognising your natural strengths gives you more than a foundation, it gives you a boost in confidence and a realisation that selling isn't one single gift but a set of component parts. When you notice you're already good at some of them, you'll see how capable you truly are, and how much more you can grow.

The Seven Habits

Habit 1: Mindset

The Seven Habits

A winning mindset consists of many things, including positivity, consistency, resilience, discipline, the ability to control your emotions, optimism and focus. The best performers don't let their mindset slip when things are difficult. They consistently apply positivity and professionalism in all situations. Customer after customer, day after day, they bring the same steady approach. That reliability is what separates good salespeople from great ones. Customers feel it. Managers notice it. And it shows up directly in the results.

Habit 2: Approach

The approach is the very first point of contact with the customer. It lays the foundations for everything that follows; a warm welcome, confident body language and an attentive presence which opens the door to trust. Done poorly, if the approach is weak or doesn't happen at all, there's nothing to build upon. The sale is lost before it even begins. However, done well, the approach lowers the customer's defences and sets the tone for a meaningful conversation.

Habit 3: Questions

Great salespeople are interested. Genuinely interested. From this comes a strong set of quality questions, the kind that help them really get to know the customer and show they care. These questions don't just fill silence, they uncover needs, spark conversation and build trust. It's this ability to ask thoughtful, well-timed questions that separates good salespeople from great ones.

Habit 4: Listening

Customers don't just want to be heard; they want to feel understood. World-class salespeople listen actively, echo back their needs and read between the lines. By showing genuine understanding, they establish a bond of trust that makes the buying process feel natural and seamless.

Habit 5: Selling the solution

Selling the solution is about having uncovered what really matters to the customer, and making that matter to you. It's about taking the time to understand what's most important to them, then matching what you've discovered with what you're about to recommend. When your suggestions clearly connect to their lifestyle, taste or priorities, both you and the customer can justify the choice with confidence. This isn't about showing products at random; it's about aligning needs and solutions so that every recommendation feels personal, relevant and genuine.

Habit 6: Conclude

Many salespeople think that 'closing' means simply asking for the order, and it's true that some lack the confidence or the right words to do this bit well. But concluding is bigger than that. It's the process of moving the customer steadily forward through the conversation so that, by the time you reach the end, the decision feels natural rather than forced. When you've built trust, checked understanding and removed doubts along the way, asking for the order almost takes care of itself, sometimes it's even unnecessary. In furniture and other considered purchases, that moment may come later, after another visit, but each positive step you create is part of concluding well. In the chapters ahead, we'll show you how to conclude brilliantly and how to ask for the order with confidence.

Habit 7: Referrals and recommendations

The sale doesn't end when the paperwork's signed. Delighted customers are your best marketers. Top performers know how to ask for referrals at the right moment, turning one happy customer into two, three or ten more.

Master these habits, and you master the process. Each one plays its part, but it's the way they fit together that transforms performance. When these habits are applied with consistency, they create momentum, conversations flow more naturally, confidence builds and results follow. The difference between an average salesperson and a great one isn't luck or personality; it's the disciplined mastery of these small, repeatable actions that, together, make selling look effortless.

The principle of marginal gains

This idea was made famous by the British Cycling Team under Sir Dave Brailsford. They didn't transform performance with one big change, but instead they identified everything that could possibly make a difference, and then did it. From cleaning bike tyres with alcohol to improve grip, to hiring a surgeon to teach riders how to wash their hands properly and avoid illness, to testing different massage gels for recovery, no detail was too small to question.[3] This disciplined approach became known as the aggregation of marginal gains; the belief that tiny, deliberate improvements in execution, made everywhere they could be, add up to extraordinary results.

Selling works the same way. A slightly warmer greeting. A better question. A more confident conclusion. On their own, these feel small. But stack them together, habit by habit, and you create the same effect: marginal gains that add up to transformational results.

In sales, these small, deliberate improvements all sit in what we call the left-hand column: your actions, behaviours and attitudes. The right-hand column is your results: the orders, the revenue, the performance numbers. Focus relentlessly on the left-hand column, and the right-hand column almost always looks after itself.

The metric that matters

When we work with sales teams, we often set a simple, measurable target: one extra order per salesperson per week.

It doesn't sound like much, does it? But let's run the numbers for a single store with six salespeople. With an average order value of £1,500 and fifty-two working weeks in the year, one extra order per person per week adds up to £468,000 in additional revenue every year. Even if you only achieved half of that, the uplift is still £234,000 a year, from just one store.

One extra order

But the real magic isn't in the number. It's in the way of thinking. By focusing on 'one extra order,' you force yourself to ask what you will need to do differently to achieve it. As a manager, you might ask which one habit should I coach more consistently across my team? As a salesperson, you might ask which one habit do I need to sharpen to tip that next conversation into a sale?

Thinking this way ties growth directly to the Seven Habits framework. You stop chasing volume and start asking which habit, if I apply it deliberately in this order, will convert that one extra sale?

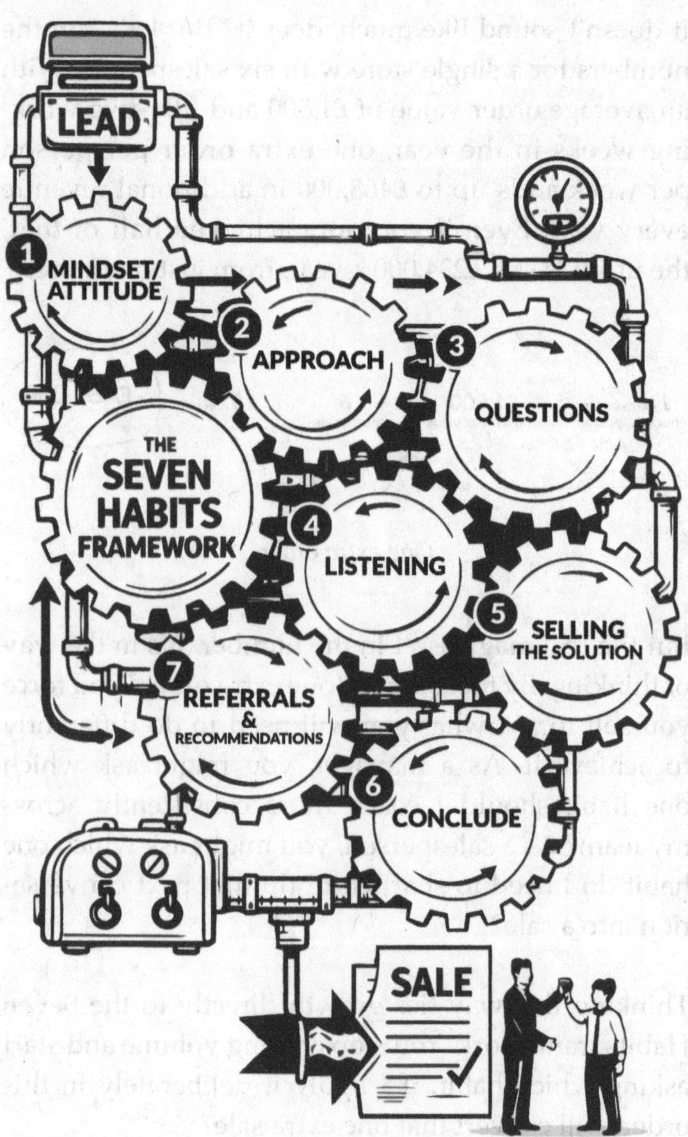

The Seven Habits Framework

The One Extra Order Question For Managers

'Which one habit, if I coached it better across my team this week, would produce one extra order?'

This is one of the simplest and most powerful questions a sales manager can ask. You don't need to reinvent your sales model or overhaul the whole store. Just focus on one habit.

Every team has its pattern. Some habits drift, others never quite take root, and some simply need re-energising. As a manager, your skill is to notice which one change would make the biggest difference this week.

To help you identify it, think through the Seven Habits and ask yourself:

- **Mindset:** Does my team start each day switched on, positive and ready to serve?
- **Approach:** Are they greeting every customer warmly, or are some approaches being missed?
- **Questions:** Are we asking enough open, discovery questions, or jumping too soon to talking about the products?
- **Listening:** Are we truly understanding the customer's situation, or just waiting to speak?
- **Selling the solution:** Are we linking what we show to what matters most to the customer?
- **Conclude:** Are we confidently asking for the order, or slipping into 'quote and hope'?
- **Referrals and recommendations:** Are we following up delighted customers and asking for introductions?

Once you've spotted the biggest opportunity, make it your coaching focus for the week. Spend time on the floor, catch people doing it right, and celebrate progress.

Here are some examples of what your one-habit focus might look like:

- Stopping the habit of giving too many choices too quickly
- Encouraging every team member to ask for the order confidently
- Preventing people from offering a quotation before the customer is ready
- Reinforcing that finance should be discussed every time, not sometimes
- Sharpening the approach so no customer is ever left unwelcomed

When you choose one habit and coach it consistently, you create visible improvement. And as each small gain takes hold, the team's confidence, results and pride grow, too.

One habit. One focus. One extra order.

2
Habit 1: Mindset

Ask any salesperson whether their mindset makes a difference, and the answer is instant and emphatic: 'Yes, absolutely, 100%, without question.' They know from experience that showing up positive and focused always leads to better sales, stronger customer relationships and more job satisfaction. Customers feel it, too. People naturally gravitate towards those who radiate warmth and energy, and they tend to move away from those who seem flat, distracted or negative.

However, although almost everyone agrees that mindset is critical, very few actively work on it. Most let their mood or circumstances set the tone. If it's raining, they expect a slow day. If a colleague makes a cutting remark, their attitude takes a downturn. If three browsers leave without buying, their energy goes with them. The result? Sales performance that swings up and down like a yo-yo.

Consider for a moment the 'negative influencer' in your store, the colleague who sighs heavily, moans about leads and complains that 'nobody's buying today.' Their words and body language don't just affect their own sales; they ripple through the team. Negativity spreads quickly. One person's slump becomes a shared atmosphere that customers can sense the moment they step inside the store.

If you can't picture the negative person in your store, it might be you!

Every day in sales should begin with the question: 'Do I have the right mindset to sell today?' It's the foundation of everything that follows. That's why we put mindset first in *The Seven Habits.* Without it, nothing else improves. Two of the biggest mindset traps I've seen in sales are complacency and cynicism.

Complacency isn't usually deliberate. It's more like a place you drift into without realising it. Think of it as like being in a long relationship where you start to take each other for granted, not because you mean to, but because you've stopped paying attention. In sales, complacency often sets in when individuals have been performing the job for so long that they simply go through the motions. They don't even realise they're there. That's why refresher training is so valuable; it wakes people up, reminds them what great selling looks like, and re-energises them to raise their game.

Cynicism is different. It's definitely negative. It's more than tiredness or drift; it's almost contempt for the craft of selling itself. Cynicism says, 'Customers aren't buying, so why bother?' It's the definition of negativity in every sense, and it's far more dangerous because it doesn't just lower standards; it actively spreads doubt and drags down colleagues as well.

Let's look at this as a wheel, called the Cycle of Development:

Cycle of Development (Mindset → Knowledge → Practice → Skill/habit)

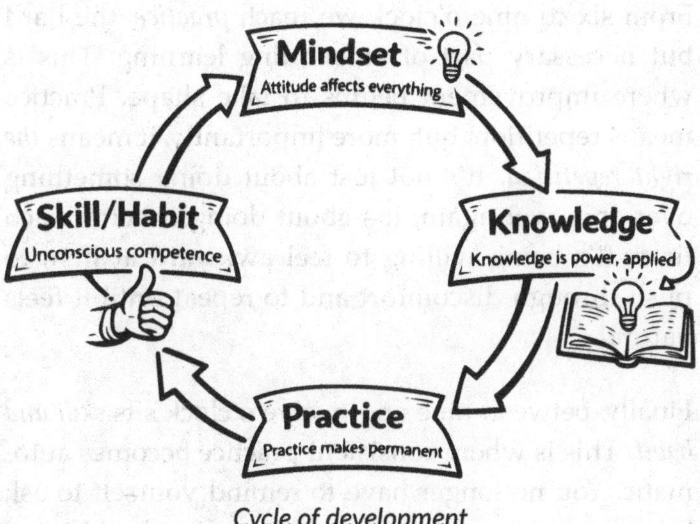

Cycle of development

Everything begins with attitude. Between twelve and three o'clock on the wheel sits *mindset*, the choice to turn up with a 'can do, want to do, will do' attitude. If that part isn't right, nothing else follows. A positive, open mindset is the ignition point for all growth. When you choose to believe in improvement, you give yourself permission to learn, change and succeed.

Moving clockwise from three to six o'clock comes *knowledge*. This is where you learn what 'great' looks like, from books, workshops, observations or coaching. People often say that knowledge is power, but that isn't quite true. *Knowledge is only power when it's applied*. Reading about the habits, tools and techniques in this book means nothing unless you take them onto the shop floor and use them with real customers.

From six to nine o'clock we reach *practice*, the hard but necessary part of embedding learning. This is where improvement begins to take shape. Practice means repetition, but, more importantly, it means *the right repetition*. It's not just about doing something over and over again; it's about doing it better each time. It's being willing to feel awkward at first, to push through discomfort and to repeat until it feels natural.

Finally, between nine and twelve o'clock sits *skill and habit*. This is where consistent practice becomes automatic. You no longer have to remind yourself to ask better questions, to pause, to listen or to build trust, it simply happens. You've hard-wired the behaviour. It's become who you are on the sales floor.

And then, of course, the wheel turns again. Each new challenge or skill starts back at attitude and mindset, the willingness to grow. That's why this model is circular, not linear. Development never stops; it loops continuously. With each turn, you build confidence, capability and consistency.

Measuring your attitude

One of the questions we ask in training is this: how do you measure attitude? Most people pause, unsure. They know attitude matters, but they don't know how to pin it down. That's when we introduce a simple idea: what if you gave it a number?

By assigning a number to your mindset, you make something emotional into something tangible. Suddenly, you can ask yourself: am I a three today, or a six, or an eight? And, more importantly, does my energy, my application and the way I come across to customers match the number I claim to be?

Many individuals find it helpful, and every team we've worked with has also found it helpful. In fact, when whole teams have agreed to use it, the results have been game changing. I've seen stores where people said, 'We're going to forget our differences, but as a team, we'll show up as an eight for every customer.' And sure enough, when they did that, performance improved across every measure.

Here's how the scale looks in practice:

- Two – Negative and draining, low energy, unmotivated, cynical, pulling others down
- Four – Complacent and coasting, not deliberately negative, just going through the motions
- Six – Neutral but inconsistent, sometimes up, sometimes down, customers feel the swings
- Eight – Positive and proactive, engaged, professional, consistent, prepared to sell
- Ten – Consistently outstanding, the bright lights of the business, lifting colleagues and customers with every interaction

When I became a manager, I used to tell salespeople to aim to be a ten every day, but here's what I discovered: most people misunderstood what a ten looks like. They thought I meant bouncing off the walls with enthusiasm, high-fiving customers at the door. That's not what we mean by being a ten, and it's not what sells furniture.

The real key is consistency. That's why I now tell people not to chase a ten, but to aim for a steady eight. Here, you're positive, professional, helpful and calm.

You're high enough to lift customers, but realistic enough to sustain it all day, every day.

That's the value of this tool. If you can put a number on your mindset and be honest about it, you can hold yourself accountable. You'll know what that number looks like in yourself, you'll spot it in your colleagues, and as a team, you can raise the bar together.

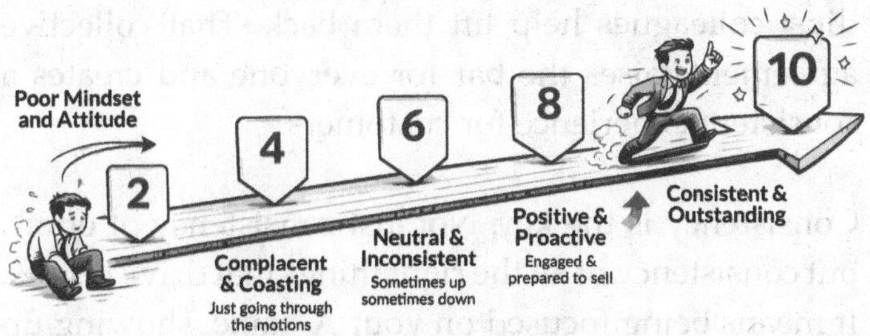

Mindset attitude scale

How to hold an eight

Consistency doesn't happen by accident; it's a choice. Maintaining an eight takes discipline and a few simple habits.

For me, the store entrance became the trigger point. Whatever was happening outside – traffic, bills, arguments, stress – I learned to leave it at the door. The moment I stepped onto the shop floor, customers deserved the best version of me. Triggers are powerful tools when you're trying to change or reinforce a habit. At any time, you can use a trigger to reset yourself positively, a signal to say, 'I'm going to try something different.' It might be a physical trigger, like crossing the threshold or a situational one, like a moment between customers, but each is a cue to re-engage and perform at your best.

In a team, it's the commitment that matters most. The most successful stores agree on a shared standard; everyone shows up as at least an eight. If someone dips, colleagues help lift them back. That collective agreement raises the bar for everyone and creates a consistent experience for customers.

Consistency is the key. Not just consistency of effort, but consistency of all the right things that drive results. It means being focused on your A-game, showing up to apply good habits deliberately and regularly. True consistency isn't ruled by feelings; it's professional. It's choosing to deliver your best even on the days you don't feel like it. The best salespeople understand this and they don't wait for motivation to strike; they create it through routine, focus and discipline. That's what sets them apart and keeps their performance steady while others fluctuate.

Of course, even the best slip sometimes. That's why great salespeople notice the slide early and act. A quick walk, a stretch, a two-minute mental reset – those small actions prevent a three o'clock slump from turning into a wasted afternoon.

So what does an eight look like? Here are the traits and habits that hold it in place:

- **Positive energy:** steady, upbeat, never flat or cynical
- **Professional presence:** body language, tone and appearance send the right signals
- **Customer focus:** attention on the person in front of you, not on distractions
- **Consistency:** the same approach, whether it's Monday morning or Saturday afternoon
- **Resilience:** quick recovery from setbacks, never carrying one 'no' into the next conversation
- **Calm confidence:** not over-the-top enthusiasm, but steady assurance that customers feel
- **Team contribution:** helping to lift colleagues if they drop, protecting the shared standard

This is where I use what I call the 'marshmallow mindset' versus the 'titanium-bar mindset.'

A marshmallow bends and folds under the slightest pressure. Push it one way, and it squishes that way. Push it the other, it squishes the other. That's how some salespeople operate. If something positive happens, their energy rises. If something negative happens, it collapses. They are entirely reactive, moving in whichever direction events push them, never holding their own shape.

Titanium is entirely different. Titanium is one of the hardest, most resilient materials we know. Drop a titanium bar from five miles up, and it won't dent or scratch. It's unshakeable, always holding its shape. That's the mentality I trained myself to adopt: the titanium-bar mentality.

Whatever happened in my day – good customers, difficult customers, big wins, tough rejections – I trained myself to remain completely unaffected. Not cold or unfeeling, but steady, consistent and resilient. That is what true bouncebackability really is.

When I first started selling, it used to take me days to bounce back from disappointment, from missing a target, losing a sale or dealing with a difficult customer. But over time, I realised how much that emotional hangover was affecting my performance. It's a classic cause-and-effect situation: the longer you dwell on the cause, the more damage you do to the effect. Between stimulus and response there's a gap, a moment where we choose how to react, and the best professionals work to make that gap shorter and shorter.

That's the key. Reduce the *dwell time*. The best salespeople don't waste energy licking their wounds, replaying frustrations or blaming circumstances. They acknowledge it, reset and move on. I remember one of our top performers, consistently at the top of the sales league for over ten years. One Saturday afternoon, about three o'clock, I saw him walking out of the washroom, face dripping with water, towel in hand. He smiled and said, 'I've just reset myself. I was having a bad day, now I'm back on it.' And guess what? He finished the day with a flurry of sales. That's what bouncebackability looks like in practice.

The best salespeople have it. Nothing phases them. Good days, bad days, happy customers, unhappy customers, ups and downs in performance; nothing changes their approach. And because they stay consistent, their results stay consistent, too.

CRITICAL CONCEPT: Behaviour Follows Belief

Quite simply, your behaviour always follows your beliefs.

If you walk onto the shop floor thinking, 'This customer isn't going to buy,' your body language, tone and effort all shift down a gear. You go through the motions. You miss signals. You rush the conversation or withdraw too quickly. And then, when the customer leaves without buying, you've created the very outcome you expected.

That's the danger of pre-judging. When you form a negative assumption before you've even said hello, you unconsciously act in ways that confirm that belief. Pre-judging is one of the most destructive habits in sales, and one of the easiest to fall into.

The antidote is to build the opposite belief, one rooted in expectancy. Instead of assuming things won't go your way, expect that they will. Expect customers to be friendly, expect great conversations, expect today to be a good day. Belief in positive outcomes changes how you show up – your posture, your smile, your patience, your tone. Train yourself to believe that every customer who walks in is somewhere on their buying journey. Maybe not today, but at some point. Holding that expectation creates a consistent approach and a steady mindset. It prevents you from swinging up and down with moods or assumptions, allowing you to treat every customer with the same energy, professionalism and focus.

Your body language always reveals your belief. You can't fake enthusiasm or conviction for long; your subconscious gives you away. That's why this principle sits at the heart of mindset, because your belief shapes your energy, your tone, your posture and, ultimately, your results.

The Power of Thought In Sales

'Every cell in your body is eavesdropping on your thoughts and acting accordingly.'

— Russ Platts, Head of Learning & Development, Furniture Sales Solutions

Russ Platts says this line often, and it's a truth that every great salesperson eventually learns: what you believe, you broadcast.

If you think someone is a 'tyre kicker,' then that belief will shape everything – before you've even said hello.

You might decide not to approach them at all, or you do so half-heartedly, already preparing yourself for rejection. You'll stand a little further away, your body closed off, your tone flat, your questions minimal. You'll only be partially committed, maybe even slightly irritated, because deep down you've already decided this isn't worth your time.

And the customer? They'll feel it. They might not be able to explain why, but something in your energy, expression or posture tells them they're not truly welcome. What happens next is predictable: the conversation goes nowhere – not because they were never going to buy, but because you never really tried.

Now flip the mindset. Imagine you know this customer has £5,000 to spend today. How do you move? How do you sound? Suddenly, your eyes brighten, your stride has purpose and your voice carries warmth and curiosity. You approach with interest, you smile naturally and you take the time to understand what matters most to them.

The difference isn't in the customer – it's in your belief.

If you genuinely believe in the value of what you sell – that your sofa will transform their home, that your protection plan offers real peace of mind – that conviction radiates through you. It shows in the way you hold eye contact, how confidently you explain options, and how attentively you listen. It's infectious.

Russ's point goes deeper than motivation, it's biology. Your thoughts trigger chemical signals – adrenaline, dopamine, cortisol – that shape your facial expressions, posture and tone. Every cell in your body literally responds to your mindset. When your thoughts are negative, your physiology follows; when they're positive, your body amplifies it.

That's why mindset isn't a 'soft skill,' it's a visible skill.

It determines whether you step forward with confidence or hang back with doubt. Whether you open doors or close them without even realising.

Every cell is eavesdropping – and every customer can hear the conversation.

The concept is simple but powerful: Belief → Behaviour → Results. When you truly hold the belief, your behaviour changes naturally and the results follow.

Here's an example I often share. Imagine your £5,000 comeback-customer drives up outside. You know them, you remember the conversation you had last time, and you believe with absolute certainty that they're back to buy. How do you behave? Your posture improves. Your face lights up. You're fully engaged, alert and ready. Every fibre of your being says: 'I am here to help this person buy.'

Now imagine applying that mindset to every single customer who walks in, not in an over-eager, pushy way, but with calm confidence and steady professionalism. The difference in your results would be staggering.

This is the essence of the critical concept: belief drives behaviour, and behaviour drives results. If you believe everyone is in the market, you behave as though they are, and your conversations change. It's the exact opposite of pre-judging customers negatively, and it's one of the simplest, most powerful shifts you can ever make in sales.

What Are We Really Selling?

Whatever you're selling, whether it's furniture, cars, houses, what you're actually selling is feelings.

Every considered purchase is logical and *emotional*. Customers don't just buy furniture – they buy how it makes them *feel*. But that feeling is created by far more than the product itself. Everything the customer experiences influences emotion: the greeting at the door, the body language of the sales team, the layout and lighting, the tone of voice, how easy the options are to understand, and how safe it feels to make a decision.

Picture the difference. A customer walks in and sees six salespeople chatting together. Their anxiety rises: 'They're all going to pounce.'

Another walks into a calm, confident atmosphere. A salesperson greets them with, 'Please make yourself at home, put your feet up. We won't follow you around, but let me just give you a couple of pointers and I'll catch up in a few minutes.'

The first store adds pressure; the second removes it. That's what great salespeople do – they turn an emotional hurdle into an emotional lift.

Our job is to manage feelings from start to finish, removing negatives and creating positives as the customer travels from uncertainty to certainty. Every smile, every question, every small reassurance moves them along that scale.

Positive feelings – what we create/encourage	**Negative feelings – what we remove/avoid**
Curious – 'I wonder what's in here?'	Anxious – 'I'm not sure I belong here.'
Interested – 'This could be what we need.'	Defensive – 'They'll try to sell me something.'
Hopeful – 'Maybe we'll finally find one we like.'	Overwhelmed – too much choice, too many decisions.
Intrigued – drawn in by design, display or story.	Intimidated – by price, jargon or process.
Comfortable – relaxed atmosphere, friendly tone.	Unsure – don't yet know who or what to trust.
Reassured (brand) – 'I've heard good things; they feel genuine.'	Confused – too much information or contradiction.
Reassured (product) – 'Yes, it'll fit; it'll last.'	Pressured – feeling hurried or watched.
Reassured (value) – 'I thought two grand; it's four, but I can see why.'	Doubtful – not sure it's worth it.
Happy – 'I like this salesperson,' enjoying the experience, picturing it at home.	Fearful – worried about making the wrong decision.
Certain and confident – all boxes ticked, decision feels right.	Doubt and fear removed – no hesitation left.

Reassurance appears at several stages of the buying journey:

- **Brand reassurance:** 'I've heard of this company – can I trust them now that I'm here?'
- **Product reassurance:** 'Will it fit? Will it last? Will it look right?'
- **Value reassurance:** 'It's more than I planned to spend, but it feels worth it.'
- **Service reassurance:** 'Will they deliver on time and sort any problems?'

Each layer of reassurance removes another layer of doubt.

As we iron out these small creases, the customer quietly confirms to themselves that they're happy with the brand, the product, the price and the delivery. By the time those feelings line up, certainty has replaced fear and the emotional close has already happened.

People buy on emotion and justify with logic.

A customer might say, 'It's double what we planned to spend,' but if they feel reassured – about quality, durability, service and support – logic quickly steps in to defend the decision: 'It'll last twice as long; it's worth it.'

Our role is to guide and encourage that inner conversation, helping them feel confident about the decision and have clear reasons to back it up later. We're not just selling products; we're managing feelings. Everything we do should reduce fear, build reassurance, create happiness and deliver certainty.

When that happens, the customer doesn't just buy a piece of furniture – they buy peace of mind and the quiet confidence that they've made the right choice.

We don't sell furniture. We sell certainty – and the feeling that buying from us was absolutely the right decision.

The transfer of enthusiasm

I worked for Lord Graham Kirkham for twenty years and I once asked him, 'What's the most important skill in selling?' His answer sums up selling better than almost anything else I've ever heard. He said, 'Selling is simply the transfer of enthusiasm.'

When you think about it, that's exactly what happens in the best sales experiences. The customer walks in carrying a mixture of curiosity, hope, excitement – and sometimes a little anxiety. Then they meet someone whose energy changes everything. Someone whose enthusiasm is so genuine and so alive that it lifts the customer up, helps them see what's possible, and makes them feel certain they're in good hands.

Russ Platts puts it another way: 'Enthusiasm is contagious – is yours worth catching?' The word itself comes from the Greek *enthousiasmos,* meaning 'the spirit within.' True enthusiasm isn't noise or hype; it's a deep inner belief. It's the spark that ignites everything else.

In furniture retail, it's rarely just enthusiasm for the product – it's enthusiasm for the project. The customer's project. Their new home. Their first apartment. Their downsize or renovation. Great salespeople become part of that story. They're almost more excited than the customer themselves. They imagine the new sofa in that living room, the dining table where the family will gather, the bed where someone will finally get a good night's sleep.

That's when selling becomes effortless. You're no longer trying to persuade; you're simply sharing your excitement about what's possible. Customers feel it. They sense that you care, that you believe, that this matters.

It's not about being loud, it's about having energy. It's not about performance, it's about passion. The most effective salespeople radiate a quiet conviction that says: this will make your life better, and I can't wait for you to experience it.

If you could bottle that feeling, you'd be a millionaire seller.

Abundance mentality: The law of attraction in action

Some salespeople succeed because they are relentlessly disciplined, they stay focused, they hold an eight and they never drift. But every so often, you meet someone different, someone rare. These people carry an air of expectation.

They expect to have great conversations. They expect to make friends. They expect customers to enjoy talking to them. And more often than not, that expectation becomes reality. Customers are drawn to them, carried along by their enthusiasm and positivity.

This is the essence of an abundance mentality – the belief that opportunities are everywhere. Instead of scarcity thinking, worrying about where the next order will come from or whether there are enough customers in the store, abundance thinkers act as though good things are already on the way. That mindset changes how they look, sound and feel to customers. They are optimistic, approachable and warm. Customers think, 'I feel comfortable with this person. I want to buy from them.'

It's also the practical expression of the law of attraction. What we focus on, we tend to amplify. Focus on scarcity, and you'll find proof that the day is quiet and nobody's buying. Focus on opportunity, and you'll start spotting chances everywhere – a new customer walking in, a returning lead, a cross-sell moment. Abundance doesn't ignore reality; it filters it through a more productive lens.

The science backs it up. Neuroscience shows that our brains are rewired by repeated thoughts and behaviours, a principle known as neuroplasticity. Every time we think, feel or act in a certain way, we strengthen the neural connections that support that pattern, making it more automatic over time. This means that practising optimism and positive expectancy literally reshapes the brain's wiring towards resilience and motivation. Functional MRI studies show that optimism activates regions such as the orbitofrontal cortex and anterior cingulate, areas responsible for decision-making, emotional control and reward anticipation.[4]

Positive psychology research supports the same finding: people who deliberately cultivate positive emotions show longer attention spans, higher creativity and better problem-solving skills. This is known as the Broaden-and-Build Theory of positive emotion.[5]

In sales terms, that's why a positive, expectant mindset helps you see opportunities others miss – a return customer walking in, a small add-on suggestion or a chance to introduce finance.

In a furniture store, this science plays out visibly. A salesperson who expects a quiet day often sees exactly that; they stand back, appear less approachable and their energy tells customers to keep walking. Meanwhile, the colleague beside them walks the floor expecting good conversations, naturally smiles more, engages sooner and spots buying signals earlier. Their belief shapes their behaviour, and their behaviour shapes the result.

The best part? Abundance isn't a personality trait, it's a choice. You can switch it on and turn it up. By deliberately carrying yourself with expectation, by deciding each morning that good conversations are waiting for you, you step into that zone more often.

Two salespeople may stand side by side in the same store, meeting the same customers on the same day. One approaches the day with tension and doubt; the other with expectation and abundance. The difference in outcomes is remarkable, same environment, completely different energy.

An abundance mentality means making the choice to expect opportunities, and expectation, more often than not, becomes a self-fulfilling prophecy.

The buying journey

Every single customer in the world who makes a considered purchase follows the same psychological journey.

A considered purchase is one in which the customer takes time to weigh things up, often because it involves a significant amount of money, whether that's a few hundred pounds, a few thousand or more. It's never an instant decision. It means considering different options, thinking through the details and often involving others in the decision-making process.

On the buying journey, we use a one-to-ten scale to identify where in the process a customer currently sits.

Think about holidays. At a one, you're daydreaming, scrolling Instagram, imagining a getaway. At a five, you've narrowed it down – city break not beach. You're comparing prices, checking if you can get the time off. At a nine, you've chosen the destination and hotel; now you just need reassurance before you click 'book.'

Furniture works exactly the same way. Customers rarely walk into a store at a ten. Most arrive somewhere between one and five. Your role as a salesperson isn't to force them to buy before they're ready. Your role is to determine where they are on their journey and move them forward.

That's the key: not every customer will buy today, but every customer is on the journey. When you understand this, you stop obsessing only over those who are ready to order immediately and start putting the same care and attention into those who are still at the early stages. This is how we turn browsers into buyers.

If you invest in the ones, twos and threes today, many of them will return later as eights, nines or tens, and because of the work you put in early, they'll buy from you.

This is where the most significant mindset shift happens. In many stores, success is judged only by what's written down that day. Managers ask, 'How much have you done today?' and salespeople beat themselves up if the answer is 'Nothing.' But what if you had five excellent conversations with early-stage customers today? They didn't buy, but they've moved forward on their journey. That's progress, and that's what tomorrow's business is built on.

So instead of asking yourself, 'What did I sell today?' start asking, 'What did I build today?' Did you build trust? Did you build momentum? Did you build relationships that will turn into orders next week or next month? Those are just as important as the orders you write today, sometimes even more so, because they create consistency.

Every quality conversation is progress. If a customer arrives at a two and leaves at a five, that's success. If they come back at a seven and you help them reach a nine, you're nearly there. Each interaction compounds.

That's the essence of the buying journey: to recognise that sales are not single events but steps along a path. Treat every customer as though they are on that journey, focus on moving them forward, and trust the process. Some sales will close on the first visit, but many more will close later, and if you've done the work, you'll be the one who writes the order.

Later in the book, when we examine the habit of asking great questions, we'll illustrate exactly how this works in practice. The right question can reveal where a customer truly is in their buying journey and help you move them forward. One of our favourite real-life examples comes from a store in Aberdeen, which we'll come to in Habit 3.

Ironing out the creases

Great salespeople know that closing starts at the start. Often, the first decisions customers make will not change, and that's why they matter so much.

Take a sofa, for example. You ask, 'Are you thinking leather or fabric?' Most people already have a preference. If they say, 'Fabric,' that's a nail-down. Most salespeople don't realise that getting a decision early on is the first solid step. It won't change after that, and that's why it's so positive on this same psychological journey. On a bed, you ask, 'Is this for yourself?' and they reply, 'Yes.' That's another nail-down. On a dining table, you ask, 'Ceramic or wood?' and they say, 'Ceramic.' That's a preference nailed.

These are anchor decisions: good for the customer, because they feel a sense of progress, and good for you, because you know you've pegged something forward.

Each nail-down irons out a crease and builds momentum for the customer. The more nail-downs you collect, the smoother the journey becomes, and the easier the conclusion feels.

And it isn't just furniture. In car sales, the same thing happens. A salesperson asks, 'Are you thinking diesel or electric?' The customer replies, 'Electric.' Nail-down. 'SUV or estate?' The customer says, 'SUV, we like sitting higher up.' Another nail-down. In technology, it's the same: 'Is this laptop for home or work?,' 'For work.' Nail-down. 'What's critical?,' 'It needs this processor.' Another decision pegged.

Whatever trade you're in, you know the key questions to ask that produce solid answers. The skill is in recognising that these aren't just bits of information, they're mini closes. They're small but significant 'yeses' that move the customer closer to the big yes.

And here's the lightbulb moment for many people in training: most salespeople confuse closing with simply asking for the order. But closing doesn't start there. Closing starts the moment you begin ironing out the creases. Every nail-down is a close in itself. By the time you've gathered enough of them, the conclusion feels easy, obvious and natural, because you've already done the work along the way.

In our training workshops, we use a simple but powerful illustration. We seat the delegates around a large U-shaped table. Up the left-hand side, across the top and down the right-hand side, we number the places from one to ten. This represents the customer's buying journey. Seat one is the first stage, when the customer is just beginning to look. Seat ten is when we close the sale and the order is signed.

Buying journey scale

Now, when we ask salespeople about the conversion rate of first-time visits, the average answer is somewhere between 20% and 50%. In other words, not everyone will buy straight away. We then ask, how many visits does it typically take before a customer makes a purchase? The typical answer is two to three visits. So, for this model, we use two-and-a-half. That means:

- During the first visit, the customer may progress from one to five.
- On the second visit, from five to eight.
- By the third (or two-and-a-half, on average), from eight to ten, and that's when the order is written.

The time with the customer is represented by that movement from one to ten. The customer themselves is like a tablecloth thrown across the table. When they first arrive, the cloth is crumpled and full of creases, doubts, questions, concerns and decisions yet to be made. Your job from the very start of the journey is to iron out those creases steadily as you go, and progress them along the journey.

Every conversation should feel like moving forward around the table, decision after decision, crease after crease. It should not be an interrogation of the customer but asking questions woven into a natural conversation, with each answer becoming a nail-down. By the time you reach nine or ten, nothing will be left unresolved, and nothing will bite you at the end, because you've already smoothed the cloth.

Here are some examples:

Sofas

- Q: 'Are you thinking leather or fabric?'
- A: 'Fabric.' Nail-down.
- Q: 'Corner group or three-and-two?'
- A: 'Three-and-two.' Nail-down.
- Q: 'Do you need quick delivery, or is timing flexible?'
- A: 'Timing's flexible.' Nail-down.

Beds

- Q: 'Is this for you or for someone else?'
- A: 'It's for us.' Nail-down.
- Q: 'What size are you thinking, 4 ft 6 in, 5 ft, or 6 ft?'
- A: '5 ft.' Nail-down.
- Q: 'Do you need a base or just the mattress?'
- A: 'We'd like a base.' Nail-down.

Dining tables

- Q: 'Are you looking for wood, glass or ceramic?'
- A: 'Ceramic.' Nail-down.

- Q: 'How many people would you like to seat every day?'
- A: 'Four.' Nail-down.
- Q: 'And for special occasions?'
- A: 'Six to eight.' Nail-down.
- Q: 'Would you prefer fixed or extending?'
- A: 'Extending.' Nail-down.

By the time you get to nine or ten on the journey, there's nothing left hanging. Every objection has already been addressed, every concern reassured, every preference nailed down. That's why concluding at the end feels natural, not forced, because the creases were ironed out steadily along the way.

Remember that closing starts at the beginning and each decision you can help the customer make thereafter is a step nearer to closing the sale – considered purchases, done properly, are not about one big yes at the end. They're about helping the customer say lots of small yeses along the way.

The salesperson's mindset reset

Switching on at the start of the day is important, but the real test of professionalism is what happens during the day.

Furniture retail is emotionally demanding. Big tickets, long decision cycles, expectations and disappointment are all part of the job. One moment you're confident and in control, the next, something doesn't go your way.

We once worked with a salesperson who was expecting a comeback at 10.30. He believed the customer was ready to proceed with around £7,000 worth of furniture. The appointment mattered. He'd built the solution, done the work and mentally banked the sale.

The customer did come back, but they didn't place the order. That moment knocked the salesperson completely off balance – not just for the rest of the morning but for the rest of the day. In fact, it stayed with him for three or four days. Every interaction after that carried the emotional weight of that one disappointment.

As it happened, the customer eventually did return and place the order. However, the damage had already been done. The salesperson's mindset had collapsed, his focus dropped and several other opportunities suffered because of it.

This is where many salespeople struggle. They don't just react to what happens, they carry it forward. A cancelled order bleeds into the next interaction with a customer. A tough phone call follows them onto the shop floor. A quiet morning turns into a flat afternoon.

Bad news from a manager sits in their head during the next conversation. None of this is deliberate. It's emotional carryover. And if you don't manage it, it quietly erodes performance.

The goal isn't to pretend disappointment doesn't exist. It's to control how long it lasts.

Professional salespeople recognise the moment something knocks them off course and reset quickly. They don't allow one moment to contaminate the next opportunity. Every customer deserves a clean slate.

A simple and highly effective tool for this comes from The Five-Second Rule, an idea popularised by Mel Robbins. When something hits you emotionally – a cancellation, hesitation, bad news or frustration – silently count down in your head – 5, 4, 3, 2, 1 – then move. Change your posture. Take a breath. Reset your face. Re-engage.[6]

That five-second window interrupts the emotional spiral before it takes hold. It stops frustration turning into sulking, disappointment turning into disengagement and expectation turning into resentment. You can't control what customers decide. You can't control when they buy. You can't control whether they change their mind. But you can control how quickly you reset.

Every new customer, phone call or conversation is a fresh opportunity. The salesperson who succeeds consistently is the one who refuses to let yesterday's disappointment, or the last interaction, dictate the next one.

Mindset control isn't about staying positive all day. It's about staying professional, feeling the moment, then letting it go.

That's how you protect your focus. That's how you stay sharp throughout the day. And that's how one missed sale doesn't cost you three more – consistency.

To sell a million pounds' worth of furniture in a year, you need to be consistent. If your average order value is around £1,500, that's roughly fifteen orders a week, allowing for holidays – and the only way you'll do that is by showing up with the same focus and energy every single day.

Consistency in face-to-face furniture sales isn't about being robotic. It's about being reliably excellent. It means you apply the same high standards whether the store is buzzing or empty, whether it's raining or sunny, whether your previous customer bought or walked out.

True consistency also demands emotional stability. Every salesperson has quieter spells – a day or two when nothing seems to land, when every 'just looking' stings a little more. The best salespeople don't crumble in those moments. They don't get dragged down by other people's moods, by negativity in the team, or by a bad run. They reset quickly, trust the process and double down on what works. They know that success over time is uneven, and that their job is to keep showing up through the dips so they can reach the peaks.

It's made up of five things:

1. Consistency of attitude: You arrive in the right state of mind, regardless of what's happening around you. You believe today will bring opportunities, and you behave accordingly.
2. Consistency of effort: You give full effort to every customer, every conversation, every quote. You don't pick and choose when to perform.
3. Consistency of focus: You stay engaged with your goals and habits. You don't drift or get distracted by what you can't control – the economy, footfall or weather.
4. Consistency of emotional response: You don't let a bad day, a difficult colleague or a slow week derail your standards. You maintain perspective, recover quickly and keep your enthusiasm intact.
5. Consistency of application of the Seven Habits: You don't just know the habits; you live them. Every day you consciously apply the principles of mindset, approach, questioning, listening, selling the solution, concluding confidently and asking for referrals. When those habits

become automatic, your consistency becomes unstoppable.

The top performers don't rely on motivation – they rely on discipline. They've built a habit of doing the small things well, every day. And when you do that for long enough, you stop chasing success and start compounding it. That's how you reach the million.

Mindset isn't just the first habit, it's the one that powers all the others. Without it, nothing else sticks.

Ensuring your mindset is right every day sets you up for great conversations with every potential customer. Part of that mindset is believing that everybody that you talk to is 'in the market.' By believing this, your approach will be more enthusiastic, interested and genuine. In Habit 2 we'll outline the perfect approach.

TIPS, TOOLS, TECHNIQUES, TRY

Tips:

- **Aim for a steady eight, not a ten.** Consistency beats hype. Customers trust calm, professional positivity more than over-the-top enthusiasm.
- **Watch for drift.** Complacency and cynicism creep in quietly. Catch them early before they become your default setting.
- **Don't pre-judge customers.** Your belief shapes your behaviour before you've even said hello. Expect a good conversation.

- **Remember what you're really selling. You're selling feelings.** Reducing fear and building reassurance is what creates certainty.
- **Think in journeys, not single events.** Not everyone is ready to buy today, but every quality conversation should move them forward.

Tools:

- **The Cycle of Development Model.** Mindset leads to knowledge, knowledge to practice, practice to skill and habit. When you slip, restart at mindset.
- **The 1–10 Mindset Scale.** Number your attitude. If you can measure it, you can manage it.
- **The stop, start, continue check.** A quick way to protect your standards, especially when the day starts to wobble.
- **The buying-journey scale (1–10).** Work out where the customer is and focus on moving them forward, not forcing a conclusion.
- **The feelings checklist.** Keep your eye on what you're creating (curiosity, comfort, reassurance, happiness, certainty) and what you're removing (anxiety, confusion, pressure, doubt).

Techniques:

- **Five-second reset.** When you dip, count 5, 4, 3, 2, 1 and move. Adjust your posture, breathe, reset your face, re-engage.
- **Titanium-bar response.** Stay steady through wins and knocks. Not cold, just consistent. Reduce the 'dwell time' after setbacks.
- **Transfer of enthusiasm.** Bring energy for the customer's project, not noise. Quiet conviction is what lifts them.

- **Iron out the creases early.** Use nail-down questions to lock in preferences and smooth doubts as you go.
- **Build reassurance in layers.** Brand, product, value, service. Each layer removes another layer of doubt until certainty replaces fear.

Try:

- **Agree the team standard.** As a store, commit to showing up as an eight for every customer, then hold each other to it.
- **Track progress, not just orders.** At the end of the day, ask, 'How many customers did we move forward on the journey?'
- **Spot your trigger phrases.** Notice when sentiments like 'nobody's buying' or 'December is dead' appear, then deliberately replace them with expectancy.
- **Run a 'belief check' before each approach.** Ask yourself: 'What am I assuming about this customer?' Then choose a better belief.
- **Practise shortening the gap.** When something knocks you, make it your goal to reset faster than last time – in seconds, not hours.

3
Habit 2: Approach

The approach is the very first 'moment of truth' in any sales interaction. It sets the tone for everything that follows. Customers decide within seconds of meeting you whether they feel comfortable, trust you and want to spend more time in your company. You may have the best products, the best finance deals or the best delivery times, but if your approach is weak, or if you don't approach at all, none of it matters.

This is the moment when the customer decides whether to open up to you or to keep their guard up. It's your chance to begin building trust and rapport, or to confirm their worst fears about salespeople. Put simply, if you don't get the approach right, everything else becomes harder.

To approach or not to approach?

One of the biggest debates in furniture sales is whether you should approach every customer. Some salespeople hesitate, convinced they will scare off potential customers. Others dive in too fast, putting customers instantly on the defensive. Both extremes are dangerous.

Some argue that customers prefer to browse undisturbed. They'll often say, 'Even I don't like being pounced on the second I walk through the door.' There's truth in that; customers don't want to feel pressured. They want space to breathe. But there's a big difference between pouncing and approaching with confidence. A confident approach is warm, natural and respectful. It acknowledges the customer without making them feel trapped.

Failing to approach is far worse. Customers left to wander on their own can quickly feel ignored. They start to think, 'Doesn't anyone care that I'm here?' Worse still, they may walk out without ever speaking to anyone.

In most cases, customers are in store for a reason. Even if they don't make a purchase that day, they are still somewhere on their buying journey. If you don't approach, you'll miss your chance to find out what the reason is, and you give up control of the sale before it's even started.

This is the real point. The whole underlying reason salespeople exist is to add value. If customers could always find what they needed on their own, there would be no need for us. Stores would just be warehouses filled with products where people help themselves and pay at a desk. But in furniture retail, it's different. Customers often don't realise the sheer range of colours, sizes, fabrics and configurations available. A good salesperson adds expertise, asks the right questions and helps customers find their perfect solution. Without you, they may never discover the product that really fits their needs, wants and lifestyle.

That's why the common excuse, 'We let customers browse, and if they need us, they'll call,' is flawed. Many customers won't call you. Instead, they may quietly conclude, 'They don't have what I'm looking for,' and leave the store. The opportunity is lost, not because the product wasn't there, but because the approach wasn't.

One of the biggest reasons salespeople hold back is fear of rejection. The irony is that rejection is more likely when the approach is poor. Approaching too quickly, with the wrong words or the wrong tone, almost guarantees the dreaded 'It's OK, we're just looking.' Over time, that becomes a vicious circle: poor approaches lead to rejection, rejection creates fear and fear leads to avoiding the approach altogether.

You should always approach but do it in the right way. Approaching customers is not optional; it's the very foundation of sales. But remember, it isn't about how quickly you do it, it's about how well you do it. A well-timed, confident and thoughtful approach makes everything that follows easier. Get the approach right, and the conversation flows. Get it wrong, or don't do it at all, and the rest of the sale becomes an uphill battle.

CASE STUDY: A Consistent Welcome

One retailer we worked with had a three-floor store, and the manager had historically found customers unattended on different levels. To fix this, they assigned the responsibility of greeting every customer as soon as they entered to a specific person. But it wasn't just a 'hello' at the door. It was a beautiful greeting: warm, welcoming and confident, followed by a fabulous journey through the store. Crucially, every single customer that entered the store received the same quality of warm welcome, so no potential customer was missed.

The salesperson stayed with the customer throughout, guiding them from floor to floor, answering questions and helping them explore the possibilities. Crucially, they also knew when to give space, stepping back at the right moments so the customer never felt pressured. The balance was perfect. One customer enters the store, and one salesperson takes ownership of the relationship.

The outcome was everything you'd want: fabulous customer experiences, more engaged conversations and consistently better results. Sales rose by more than 20%, not because the store changed its products or prices, but because every customer was guaranteed a consistent, positive and professional start to their journey.

Pre-approach: First impressions and the danger of pre-judging

Pre-approach is about being in the right mindset and as ready as possible before the customer even steps into the store. It's preparing yourself physically, mentally and in every other way possible to make the best impression the moment they arrive.

Salespeople are often guilty of pre-judging customers, watching them approach the store and deciding 'they're not buying today,' just as customers are just as busy pre-judging us.

Think of the glass door or large windows at the front of your store. Remember: **'the glass works both ways'**. You might be watching them, but they are also watching you. What do they see? Five salespeople stood together chatting. Someone sat behind a desk, head down. One person near the entrance, arms folded and a scowl on their face, 'ready' to greet them. All of these images shape the customer's first impression, often before a single word is spoken. It's an old adage, but a true one: you never get a second chance to make a first impression. Research from Princeton University found that people form an impression of someone's trustworthiness, competence and approachability in as little as one-tenth of a second (100 milliseconds).[7]

That's why the pre-approach matters. Once your mindset is in the right place first thing in the morning, the next step is to make sure your body language and behaviour tell the same story.

The most powerful physical pre-approach technique is to be visibly busy with nonthreatening activities. Hoovering, dusting, cleaning, moving stock, checking tickets or even walking with a piece of paper as though you're on a mission; all of these create the impression of natural busyness. You can use a 'prop,' the hoover, the duster, a pen, a clipboard, anything that shows you're occupied. The very best salespeople aren't genuinely focused on the task; they're using that prop deliberately to appear relaxed, calm and nonthreatening. It looks like you're focused on work, but really you're creating the perfect conditions for customers to feel comfortable. The busier you appear, the more likely customers are to come to you, tapping you on the elbow to ask for help. This doesn't mean you stand around waiting to be approached, far from it. Being visibly busy keeps you alert and observant, ready to spot visual or audible buying signals so you can time your approach perfectly.

Of course, this isn't by accident. The best salespeople use these tasks deliberately, doing them in the vicinity of the entrance or where customers are browsing. That way, when the customer looks ready, you're already close enough to make contact in a warm, natural way. It feels unforced for them and deliberate for you, the perfect balance.

The best salespeople don't start selling when the customer walks in – they start connecting. Before they think about products, they think about people. Before they talk, they listen. Before they sell, they build trust. And it's here that one of the simplest, most effective lessons I ever heard comes from, courtesy of Graham Kirkham's early days in business: pal them up.

Pal them up

There was a salesperson called Jim – one of Graham's first recruits – and he was known for one simple thing. He could 'pal them up.'

That was Graham's phrase. Jim didn't like fancy sales language. He thought words like *rapport* were too clever for their own good. Jim didn't 'build rapport,' he just made friends with people. He'd talk to customers about where they'd driven from, what they were up to that day, what their plans were for the weekend. Usually, nothing at all to do with furniture. There was no technique, no trick – just a genuine interest in people.

Jim had that natural ability to make people feel comfortable. He wasn't rushing them, sizing them up or waiting for his turn to talk. He made it feel like he had all the time in the world. And once people relaxed, they liked him – and when they liked him, they trusted him.

That's what 'pal them up' means. It's not a tactic. It's a mindset. It's about starting a conversation as a person, not as a salesperson. Forget the product for a few minutes and focus entirely on the person in front of you. Ask where they've travelled from, what brings them in, whether they've bought from you before. Laugh. Listen. Connect.

When you do that sincerely, something shifts. The customer stops feeling guarded and starts to enjoy the experience. They open up about what they're really looking for, what they like and what's holding them back.

It's the same principle that Dale Carnegie wrote about in *How to Win Friends and Influence People*: people buy from people they like – and people like people who take a genuine interest in them.[8]

Jim might have looked 'old-fashioned' by today's standards, but he outsold nearly everyone else. Not because he was slick or persuasive, but because he was authentic. He sold more by being friendly than others did by being forceful.

So, when you're next on the shop floor, remember Jim. Before you sell a product, *pal them up*.

Major time and minor time

In sales there are only two types of time: *major time* and *minor time*.

Major time is any time spent with a prospect, that is someone who is not yet a customer. Minor time is everything else – tidying, straightening displays, checking emails, moving tickets, talking, organising, or 'just finishing something off.'

Great salespeople understand this instinctively: when a potential customer is in the building, major time always beats minor time. Tasks can wait. Customers can't. This doesn't mean pouncing or rushing people, but it does mean being mentally and physically available, ready to engage and prioritising the customer over activity that feels productive but doesn't produce results.

This links to a simple but powerful question: *which is the most important order of the day?*

The answer is the first one. The first order sets the tone for everything that follows. If you don't write an order before lunch, pressure starts to build. Frustration creeps in. You begin trying harder, forcing conversations and that pressure leaks into the customer experience. Get ready and get yourself a win with that first order.

The second most important order of the day is the last. Many people mentally switch off by mid-afternoon. The best salespeople stay switched on into what we call *Fergie time* – playing beyond the whistle. That last order sends you home on a high and carries momentum into the next day.

Major time creates sales. Minor time supports it – but only when it's in the right place.

The perfect first approach

The first approach is the foundation of the entire sales journey. Get this moment right and everything else becomes easier. Miss it, delay it or get it wrong, and every stage after feels like hard work.

That's why people call selling a numbers game. Not because customers are numbers but because the more first approaches you execute well, the more doors you open to trust, rapport and real conversations.

A great first approach isn't luck. It's structure. It's made up of five parts.

1. Mindset first: believe they're in the market

Before you say a word, your belief is already talking.

If you genuinely believe that everyone who walks in is in the market, maybe not today, but at some point, you will naturally show up differently. Your posture, your tone, your patience and your interest all rise. You look like someone worth buying from.

If you pre-judge them as 'just looking' or 'not buying,' you will unknowingly communicate that too. You will hold back. You will ask weaker questions. You will disengage earlier. And the customer will feel it.

Your belief drives your behaviour. Your behaviour drives the result.

So the first rule of the perfect approach is simple: walk towards every customer with expectancy. Assume a good conversation is waiting to happen.

2. Timing: don't miss the moment

The first approach has a window. Leave it too long and the customer settles into the store without you. They become harder to engage, and you have to work twice as hard to restart the relationship.

Approach early enough to be helpful, but not in a way that feels like a pounce. The aim is not to trap them. The aim is to make them feel welcome and relaxed.

Customers don't come in hoping to be ignored. They come in hoping to feel safe.

3. The opening line: welcome them, don't shut them down

Welcome means, 'I'm pleased to see you.'

Think about greeting someone at your home. You open the door with warmth and you mean it. In store, it should feel the same. Too often customers walk in and see the opposite, someone scowling or someone looking at the clock near closing time, sending the message: 'You're an inconvenience.'

The simplest and most effective greeting is still the best: 'Good morning,' or, 'Good afternoon, how are you today?' Say it with a smile and a calm confidence.

What you want to avoid are the dead-end questions that kill conversation before it starts: 'Are you OK there?,' 'Do you need any help?' or 'Give me a shout if you need me.' They don't open anything. They give the customer one easy exit: 'We're fine, thanks.'

And that leads to the classic problem in furniture retail. A manager asks, 'Have you spoken to that customer?' and the salesperson says, 'Yeah, they're OK.' But 'they're OK' often just means they asked, 'Are you OK?' and the customer said 'Yeah.'

That isn't a first approach. That's a tick-box.

The better coaching question, and the better standard, is this: 'What do you know about that customer?' Because the job of the first approach is not to get an order. It's to break the ice and start gathering information.

4. Break the ice: one simple rapport question

The first approach should feel natural and human. A short rapport question breaks tension and helps the customer relax.

Simple lines work brilliantly: 'Where have you travelled from today?' or 'Have you been in to see us before?' If they've been before, you might say, 'Welcome back. What brings you in this time?' If they haven't, 'Welcome in. Let me quickly explain how we work.'

That small connection changes everything. It creates comfort. It creates trust. It gives you something real to build on.

Remember, most customers have already researched online. Many will tell you exactly what they've come to see. If someone says, 'We've come to see the XYZ model,' that's a gift. It gives the conversation direction immediately.

5. Add value, then step back without disappearing

A good first approach gives space, but it doesn't vanish. Sometimes, adding one useful nugget early stops a customer walking straight back out again. It also creates reassurance and reduces uncertainty, which is what we're really selling.

For example: 'Just so you know, this corner group can be built the other way round, or as regular sofas,' or, 'We've also got easy payments and finance options if that helps?'

Then, when it's right to give them room, do it with structure. The wording matters: 'Lovely to meet you. My name's Adam. I'll let you get your bearings. Please make yourself at home, and I'll catch up with you in a couple of minutes to see how you're getting on.'

That sentence does four things. It reassures them. It gives them your name. It gives them space. And it sets up the second approach.

It also keeps you in control of the journey without hanging on their leg. You're not following them around, but you're not abandoning them either. You're staying available, professional and present.

And if it's appropriate, you don't always have to step away at all. Some customers want guidance there and then. If they're engaged, asking questions or clearly on a mission, you can continue the journey with them around the store naturally.

The perfect first approach isn't one fixed script. It's a structured start: right mindset, right timing, the right opening words, a quick ice-breaker, then either guide or give space, but always with an agreed next step.

Handling 'We're just looking'

Even when you've mastered the perfect first approach, there will be plenty of times when the customer still says, 'It's OK, we're just looking.' This is one of the most common objections in sales and one of the most important to handle well.

Why does it happen? Often, it's because the salesperson has asked a closed question, such as 'Are you OK there?' or 'Do you need any help?' The customer responds with the easiest defence they know: 'We're just looking.' Sometimes it's delivered politely, but at other times it can feel abrupt, defensive or even rude.

The key is this: the first rule of handling an objection is to welcome it or, at the very least, acknowledge it. In this case, we welcome it.

So, when the customer says, 'It's OK, we're just looking,' your response is simple: 'Of course!' And say it with a smile. It's in the spirit of, 'Of course, that's exactly where you should start. That's the best place to start.' Add a touch of humour if it suits you: 'Of course, we don't charge for looking on a Tuesday or Wednesday.' Whatever works for you, the point is to accept it with warmth and move on.

This stops you from getting emotionally dented by the response. Many salespeople take 'We're just looking' as a personal rejection. They feel it emotionally, lose confidence and give up. However, the customer isn't rejecting you; they're simply protecting themselves. When you welcome it with 'Of course' and a smile, you show you're comfortable, and you demonstrate one of the most essential skills in sales: becoming emotionally detached from the outcome. When you detach, you stop feeling threatened and start making the customer feel at ease.

One of my favourite real-life examples of this came when I was in one of my Liverpool stores. A customer stormed in, very aggressive. The salesperson, standing ready for the next approach, greeted him warmly: 'Good morning, sir.' The customer snapped back in a strong Liverpudlian accent: 'F*!k off, mate.' Without blinking, the salesperson replied, 'I will in a minute, but let me just tell you how the store works.' Brilliant. Perfect handling of the worst possible rejection you could receive from a customer. It was what we call a pattern interrupt. The customer didn't expect it, and he was completely flummoxed when the salesperson showed total composure and emotional detachment from the outcome. Most other salespeople would have been offended, defensive or dented by that kind of response. But this salesman, because of his life experience (he'd been in the army), was able to handle it brilliantly.

That example stuck with me. It was a lightbulb moment, a perfect demonstration of composure, confidence and control under pressure. It's exactly where the 'Of course' approach came from, and it still stands as one of the best examples I've ever seen of turning hostility into humour and disarming tension with total professionalism. The best bit was that, half an hour later, the salesperson had sold the customer a huge corner group at £2,695!

BUYING SIGNALS: What To Look For And Listen For

For many salespeople, especially those new to the floor, the fear is that they only get one chance at the first approach. In reality, customers give multiple opportunities to re-approach. Recognising buying signals, the visual or verbal cues that tell you a customer is interested, is more important than trying to nail the first line every time.

In fact, it's often better to make a considered second approach at the moment of a buying signal than to rush in with a clumsy first one. Experienced salespeople do this instinctively. For newer salespeople, it takes practice. And remember, one of the biggest traps in retail is the institutionalised habit of staying behind the desk. If you want to succeed, you need to be on the floor, spotting and acting on these signals.

Here are some of the most common examples of buying signals:

- Sitting on a product for more than a minute. They're not just resting. They're testing the comfort, picturing it in their own homes.
- Measuring with a tape or phone. Browsers don't measure. Customers do it because they're checking it against their space.
- Checking swatches or finishes closely. Feeling fabrics, holding colours to the light, comparing options. They're visualising the match with their décor.
- Taking photos. Whether it's the product, the ticket or the swatches, the photos indicate that they want to think about it later or show it to someone else.
- Coming back to the same item. A second look is rarely casual. It's intent building.
- Asking about delivery or availability. Nobody cares about lead times or stock unless they're already considering ordering.
- Discussing finance or price. When couples talk about affordability or monthly payments with each other, you should be ready to help.

- Involving another person in the decision. Pointing out details to a partner, parent or friend is a sign that they're seeking validation before moving forward.
- Throwaway comments to each other. These are often the most valuable. Listen for things like:
  - 'I wonder if they do this in XYZ.'
  - 'I don't like the cushion, it's too soft.'
  - 'It's nice, but I'm not sure about the arms.'

These aren't negatives; they're openings. They don't know that the cushion can be made of foam or fibre, or that there are multiple arm styles. This is your chance to step in and add value.

The key takeaway is this: buying signals aren't always obvious. They can be subtle, easy-to-miss comments or quiet behaviours. But each one is an invitation. If you're tuned in and ready to act, they give you a natural way to engage and move the conversation forward.

The second approach: A gift

We left the first approach with, 'My name's Adam, I'll catch up with you in a minute to see how you're getting on.' Now it's time to deliver on that promise.

The second approach usually comes two, three, maybe four minutes later. During that time, you stay in the vicinity, keeping a close eye on the customer.

You're looking for visual buying signals and listening for audible ones, too.

These signals are everywhere, a customer looking closely at swatches, reading a ticket, trying out the furniture, taking a photo of the label, or discussing options with their partner. The golden rule is to time your re-approach in sync with those signals.

This is where the power of the first approach really shows itself. Because you said, 'I'll catch up with you in a minute,' the customer expects you to return. It feels natural. You've given yourself an open invitation. Without that, if all you'd said was, 'Give me a shout if you need any help,' then coming back around the corner two minutes later feels like pestering, and customers often see it that way.

When you do re-approach, you've got two good options depending on the situation. If the customer looks relaxed and open but not yet showing a clear buying signal, simply return with a warm, open question: 'How are you getting on?' It feels natural, expected and comfortable, because you promised to come back, the customer won't feel stalked; they'll simply feel looked after. You said, 'I'll catch up with you in a couple of minutes to see how you're getting on,' and that's exactly what you've done. It delivers on your promise, builds trust, and opens the conversation again in an easy, unforced way.

Gift, benefit, follow-up question: You'll notice with every gift of information that we give the customer, we also tell them the benefit and follow it up with an open question that encourages the customer to share more, and also gains us invaluable information that will help us nail-down various elements that are important to the customer.

In the examples below, the customer is already showing a clear buying signal, and that's the moment to go in with what we call a gift. This is where you share a small piece of helpful information that matches what they're focused on and immediately invite them to respond.

If they're looking at swatches: 'Just to let you know, we do this in several colours, so you can choose the colour that's best for you. What colour were you thinking of?'

If they're sitting on a sofa: 'Just to let you know, what we've got on display is a four-seater, a two-seater and a cuddler chair. We also do this in a three-seater, a standard chair and even as a corner group, so you can choose the combination that works best for you. What combination were you thinking of?'

If it's a promotional item: 'Just to let you know, this one is in today's promotion. You're saving £400 on that. What pieces were you thinking of?'

Or another promotion line: 'This one's got £500 off in today's promotion, so you're getting a great saving. What combination were you thinking of? What size were you thinking of?'

The most powerful gift of all is to go in with a saving. For this last example, if they reply, 'We were thinking of a three-and-two,' you can respond, 'Perfect. In that case, you'd be saving £900 today across the set.'

In furniture stores, promotions, sales and price reductions are common, and as salespeople, we can become desensitised, even numb, to the savings. Because we run from one event to another, it can start to feel like we're never really selling at the higher price, even though we must have done to remain compliant and legal. The danger is that we take these savings for granted. Yet for the customer, this is often the single most powerful motivator. It's essential to highlight it confidently and naturally: 'Just to let you know, you're saving £500 on that sofa today.' You're not saying it's *only* for today, but you're suggesting timeliness, which builds positive urgency and energy.

This approach also massively reduces the likelihood of needing to discount later. When the customer later asks, 'What's the best price you can do on that?' you can simply reply, 'I don't mind you asking, but don't forget, you're already saving £500 today.' Most customers only have one objection in them, and we've seen discounting almost completely eradicated when whole teams commit to this renewed belief and conviction in the genuine savings their customers are making. It's a powerful reframe, both in the salesperson's mind and in the customer's.

Because I want to buy one

Once you've shared your gift, whether that's a price saving, a feature or a benefit, the next step is to pause and shut up! The silence is critical. Don't rush to fill it. Let the customer process what you've just said. Almost every time, they'll respond with their first big question. That question is not casual; it's a buying signal.

Because I want to buy one

Whatever the customer asks at this stage, add the phrase *'because I want to buy one'* in your own mind. This reframing helps you recognise intent instead of resistance.

For example:

'Do you do it in purple?' *(because I want to buy one)*

'Can I get it delivered on Saturday?' *(because I want to buy one)*

'What's the delivery time on this one?' *(because I want to buy one)*

'Do you do it in leather as well as fabric?' *(because I want to buy one)*

'Will it fit through a standard doorway?' *(because I want to buy one)*

Once you start hearing every question with that in mind, your perception changes. You stop getting defensive and start engaging. It turns ordinary questions into opportunities to move the sale forward.

When I first heard this reframing technique, it completely changed my perspective. I realised how defensive I'd been when customers asked questions I thought were just them being awkward, trying to stall or even looking for excuses not to buy. Once I understood that every question is really a buying signal, it was a lightbulb moment. Whenever I share this idea with salespeople, they get the same reaction. Suddenly, they see those 'annoying' questions for what they really are: customers saying, in their own way, 'I want to buy one.'

The second approach in action

A couple are sitting on a sofa, testing it out. The salesperson, who earlier said 'I'll catch up with you in a minute,' returns, timing it with the buying signal of them trying the furniture and reading the ticket.

SALESPERSON: 'Just to let you know, this one's in today's promotion. You're saving £500 on this sofa. What combination were you thinking of?'

CUSTOMER: 'We were thinking of a three-and-two.'

SALESPERSON: 'Perfect. In that case, you'd be saving £900 today across the set.'

(Pause – the salesperson holds the silence, smiling and staying relaxed. The couple processes what they've just heard.)

CUSTOMER: 'What's the delivery time on this one?' *(In the salesperson's mind: because I want to buy one.)*

SALESPERSON: 'That depends on the fabric you choose. In the standard range, you're looking at about six weeks. Were you leaning more towards fabric or leather?'

Customer: 'Definitely fabric. Do you do it in a light grey?' *(In the salesperson's mind: because I want to buy one.)*

Salesperson: 'Yes, light grey is one of the most popular colours. It's available in this range, and I can show you some swatches. What shade of grey are you picturing for your living room?'

The ping-pong effect

What's happening here is what we call a ping-pong effect. You've gone in with a gift: useful information about a saving or a feature. The customer has responded. You've followed with a natural, open question. They've answered again. And so, the conversation bounces back and forth.

Ping-pong creates flow. It feels natural, not forced. Most importantly, it makes the customer feel part of the process rather than feeling like the salesperson is trying to 'do something to them.' That shared rhythm is what builds comfort, trust and momentum toward the sale.

The early introduction of easy payments, an essential part of your approach

A world-class approach should include three elements: a warm welcome, help navigating the store and the early mention of easy payment options, if they're available.

Why? Because many customers walk away when the total price feels out of reach. By introducing payment options early, you build a bridge that makes the purchase possible.

I'll never forget the first time I experienced this myself. In the 1970s, my dad inherited a Bang & Olufsen TV, and from then on, that brand had a special place in my mind. Years later, as a young father, I stood outside their Southport store staring longingly through the window, certain I couldn't afford to shop there. At the time, there were no visible signs in the store about finance, and I knew I couldn't afford the whole amount. From a pride point of view, I was never going to ask if they did finance. Many people fall into that category.

Five years later, having been promoted at work, I went back and this time went in. I admired the sleek TVs, some priced like cars, and stopped at one that silently swivelled on its base with the touch of a remote. I had no intention of buying that day; on the buying scale, I was only a one or a two, but I'd always dreamed of owning one. However, we were having an extension built, so in my subconscious mind I knew that we'd need some kind of TV.

As I was staring longingly at the TV, it silently began to swivel. I was delighted and looked around for an explanation. The salesperson came over, remote control in hand. He said, 'It's brilliant, isn't it? We've sold six this week.' I asked how (a little bit jealous of these buyers, given that I'd been admiring this brand for years), and he replied: 'We offer interest-free finance. Just a 10% deposit, and you spread the rest over twelve months, no catches, no penalties, same as cash.'

In that moment, it was as if the TV I'd always wanted was on the other side of a ravine and he'd shown me how to reach it.

Twenty minutes later, I left with a contract in my hand.

I would not have asked if they did finance because I wouldn't want the salesperson to think that I couldn't afford it – this is why, as salespeople, we need to bring it up every time, not wait for the customer to ask, because in most cases, they won't.

That is the power of introducing easy payments early. It doesn't push customers away; it brings their dream into reach.

Why it matters

Independent research and years of experience in-store consistently show the power of offering easy payment options. This isn't just interest-free; it includes 'buy now, pay later,' low-interest credit or flexible monthly payment plans. Whatever the exact product, the benefits are clear:

- Customers are four times more likely to purchase on their first visit if easy payment options are clearly and confidently offered.
- The average spend in the UK on easy payments is roughly 50% greater than on cash purchases.
- Add-on attachment increases because customers justify extras as part of their monthly payment: 'It's only £100 a month, and that includes product protection.'
- Loyalty and repeat visits double because customers think, 'They offered easy payments last time, I'll just go back and do it the same way again.'

When you become comfortable discussing easy payments, whether at the start of the conversation, the end or both, you remove doubt, open the customer's mind and give yourself the best possible chance of converting them at any stage of the buying journey.

When and how to introduce easy payment options

Easy payments should never be a hidden extra; they should be a natural part of every sales conversation.

The key is to build the habit of introducing them at three points:

1. At the start: As you step away after your first approach, make it part of your 'just to let you know' line:

'Oh, just before I forget, folks, we also do easy payment options. That's interest-free over two, three, or sometimes even four years, or low monthly payment plans up to four years. For example, on around £3,000, with roughly a 20% deposit (£600), your ballpark payments would be, interest-free, about £100 a month over two-and-a-half years. Low monthly payment options would be around £25 per £1,000, so about £75 a month over four years. Just thought I'd let you know.'

Then walk away as if it makes no difference to you. Be light, be relaxed, almost blasé. That way, the customer feels no pressure, but they've clocked it, and it will often come back later: 'You mentioned finance earlier, how much does it work out?'

2. In the middle: If the customer shows interest or asks a price-based question, naturally drop it back in. Remind them that easy payment options exist and keep it simple. The customer doesn't need percentages; they just need an idea of affordability. Give them a ballpark figure if they've made a selection, for example, 'What you're looking at is about £120 per month, starting a month after delivery, what do you think?'

Never ask, 'Would you like me to give you some payment options?' because that gives them the opportunity to say no.

3. At the end – always: Even if the customer says they're going away to think about it, introduce easy payments as part of your wrap-up. This is where it works as an assumptive close. For example: 'Just while you're here, let me give you all your payment options. Your order is £3,000. That would be a £600 deposit, with the balance due before delivery. Alternatively, we offer interest-free for up to three years on this range, which is about £100 a month, or the lowest monthly payment option at around £75 a month over four years.'

Always give the ballpark, round figures. Customers don't want a calculator; they want a feel for affordability. Use these easy examples:

Total spend	Typical deposit (20%)	Interest-free example	Low-interest 9.9% example (£25 / £1k pm)
£1,000	£200	£33/mo over 2.5 years	£25/mo over 4 years
£2,000	£400	£67/mo over 2.5 years	£50/mo over 4 years
£3,000	£600	£100/mo over 2.5 years	£75/mo over 4 years
£5,000	£1,000	£167/mo over 2.5 years	£125/mo over 4 years

You don't need to provide every permutation; just simple, confident, ballpark figures will suffice. Keep it clear, straightforward and customer friendly.

Here's the discipline, you've got to know your numbers. Every salesperson should be able to confidently give these ballpark monthly payments on £1,000, £2,000, £3,000 or £5,000 without hesitation. The moment you pause, fumble or reach for a calculator, the confidence is gone. Learn the easy maths, know your examples cold and make easy payments a natural part of every conversation.

Easy payments aren't pressure; they're possibility.

TIPS, TOOLS, TECHNIQUES, TRY

Tips:

- **Approach is the first moment of truth.** Customers decide in seconds whether they trust you and want to spend time with you, so the start sets the tone for everything.
- **Warmth and confidence beat speed.** Customers do not want to be pounced on, but they do want to be acknowledged and made to feel welcome.
- **Approaching is better than not approaching.** When customers are left alone, they can feel ignored and walk out without ever speaking to anyone.
- **Your job is to add value.** Customers often do not realise the range of sizes, colours, fabrics and configurations available, and your expertise helps them find the right solution.

- **Pre-judging kills performance.** Customers are judging you through the window before you speak, and if you pre-judge them as 'not buying,' your body language will give it away.

Tools:

- **Pre-approach 'non-threatening busyness.'** Use a harmless prop (hoover, duster, tickets, clipboard) to look calm, occupied and approachable while staying alert to what's happening.
- **Buying signals checklist.** Look and listen for swatches, measuring, checking tickets, taking photos, sitting and testing, returning to the same item, delivery talk, price talk, involving a partner, and throwaway comments.
- **Gift, benefit, question framework.** 'Just to let you know...' plus the benefit, followed by an open question that gathers information and keeps the conversation moving.
- **Easy payments ballparks.** Know the simple anchor figures and a typical deposit, so you can talk confidently about affordability without reaching for a calculator.
- **Manager coaching question.** Replace 'Have you spoken to them?' with 'What do you know about that customer?' so the team is driven towards information and value, not tick-box contact.

Techniques:

- **Handle 'We're just looking' with acceptance.** A warm 'Of course' and a smile removes tension and keeps you emotionally detached from the outcome.
- **Second approach timing.** Stay nearby, then re-approach when you see a buying signal so it feels natural and perfectly timed.

- **Two re-approach options.** Either deliver your promise with 'How are you getting on?,' or go straight in with a gift matched to what they are doing.
- **Pause and shut up.** After the gift, hold the silence. Let the customer process, then listen for the question that follows.
- **'Because I want to buy one' reframing.** Add this sentence in your head after every customer question so you hear intent instead of resistance and stay positive and engaged.

Try:

- **Write three 'just to let you know' gifts.** One for swatches, one for configuration, one for a promotion saving, each ending with an open question.
- **Practise the 'Of course' response ten times.** Roleplay 'We're just looking' until your tone stays calm, warm and automatic.
- **Drill buying signals on the shop floor.** For one shift, do nothing except spot and list signals you saw, then discuss them as a team.
- **Memorise the payment anchors.** Be able to quote ballparks for £1k, £2k, £3k and £5k without hesitation, including a typical deposit.
- **Run the 'one customer, one owner' exercise.** For a day, assign each new customer to one salesperson who guides, steps back at the right moments, then re-engages, aiming for a consistent welcome every time.

4 Habit 3: Foundational Questions

Selling isn't telling. If all we had to do was tell customers the details of a product to get them to buy, we'd all be smashing targets every month. But simply downloading information isn't enough. As Tony Robbins put it: 'Successful people ask better questions, and as a result, they get better answers.'[9]

Think of it like going to the doctor. If you say you have a headache and they just prescribe painkillers, they might miss something serious. You'd expect them to ask questions first. Where is the pain? How long have you had it? What sort of pain is it? The more they ask, the better they can diagnose your condition and recommend the proper treatment.

That same logic applies to selling. Great salespeople ask thoughtful, relevant questions, not just to tick a box, but because they genuinely want to understand the customer. When you understand the customer, you can recommend the right solution.

Asking great questions isn't about interrogating the customer or overwhelming them. It's about focusing on the quality of the question, its relevance and when and how we ask it. Asking the right questions at the right time helps the customer think more clearly and make better decisions.

It's tempting to think that customers expect us to talk, explain and persuade. But customers don't buy because of what you say, they buy because of how you make them feel.

That's the mindset shift needed to move from the default position of 'I need to talk' to 'I need to learn.' Good questions put the customer at the centre of the conversation. They encourage openness, uncover needs, clarify motivation and build trust.

This habit isn't about having a rigid script. It's about having a toolbox of question types you can draw from naturally, depending on the customer and the moment.

Customer FAQs

Every salesperson hears the same FAQs again and again. Handled badly, they become barriers. Handled well, they create opportunities.

If we know a handful of key questions that come up repeatedly, there's no reason not to be prepared for them.

FAQ 1: 'When does your sale finish?'

In a promotion-driven furniture store, this question comes up constantly. It can appear very early in an interaction, after you've spent twenty minutes with a customer, or even when you're already with someone else and another customer taps you on the shoulder to ask it.

Although it can sound like a delaying tactic, it is almost always a buying signal. What the customer is really asking is: 'I'm interested, but how long have I got before I need to commit?'

The first thing to do is *welcome the question*. Opening with 'Great question' gives the customer favourable attention. Psychologically, it reassures them that they're thinking in the right way and that this is a sensible thing to ask.

You must then answer the question directly.

Customer: 'When does your sale finish?'

Salesperson: 'Great question. The main event runs until the third of March. However, we also have offers within offers in store. That can include things like size upgrades, power upgrades, free bedding, reduced delivery or limited availability on certain lines. While you're here...'

At this point, clearly outline what you will do next: 'Show me what you're looking at, and I'll tell you a little bit about the product itself. I'll double-check availability on the exact option you're interested in. And I'll double-check today's sale price or promotion so you know exactly where you stand.'

As you say this, gesture naturally towards the product and begin walking with the customer, finishing with an open question to keep the conversation moving.

The structure is simple, confident and reassuring. You've answered their question, introduced urgency without pressure and smoothly transitioned back into the sales journey.

FAQ 2: 'When does your sale start?'

This is the flip side of FAQ 1 and, again, it's a buying signal. You'll usually hear this when you're not currently in a promotion, often during price establishment. The customer is clearly interested, but they're looking for reassurance around value and timing.

What they're really saying is: 'I like this, but am I paying the right price, or should I wait?'

As with all buying signals, the first step is to *welcome the question*, opening with 'Great question.' You then need to reframe the conversation away from waiting for a sale and back towards value, without becoming defensive.

Customer: 'When does your sale start?'

Salesperson: 'Great question. Just to let you know, everything here at Adam's Furniture Emporium is built up to a quality, not down to a price. While you're here...'

You then clearly outline what you're going to do next: 'Show me what you're looking at, and I'll tell you a little bit about the product itself. I'll double-check availability on that exact option. And I'll double-check our best price on that particular product for you.'

That final line is important. It keeps the conversation open and gives you flexibility. In some businesses, it allows you to capture details for a future promotion. In others, it opens the door to a better price there and then, if that's appropriate. And sometimes, the best price genuinely is the ticket price. Either way, you've moved the customer forward instead of letting them mentally park the decision.

As you say this, gesture naturally towards the product and begin walking with them, finishing with an open question to keep the conversation flowing.

The key is that you don't argue with the question, and you don't shut it down. You acknowledge it, reframe it and use it as a bridge back into a meaningful sales conversation.

FAQ 3: 'What grade of leather is this?' or 'What type of leather is it?'

When customers ask this, it's a buying signal. They like leather but want reassurance. Many salespeople over-complicate it with jargon. Keep it simple.

Sometimes a customer will mention a 'category 86' or 'category 94.' That usually came from another salesperson and probably confused them. If they're asking, it means another store's explanation stopped them buying, which is great news for you, because now you can help them think clearly.

Customer: 'What grade of leather is this?'

Salesperson: 'Great question. Just to let you know, all our leather sofas are 100% leather all the way around.' (Only say this if it's true.) 'We just give them different finishes depending on lifestyle. So, if you don't mind, let me ask you a few questions about your lifestyle and we can find the right leather for you and your family.'

This simplifies the options for the customer and makes them focus on the right finish for their lifestyle, not get into jargon like 'aniline, semi-aniline or corrected-grain.'

FAQ 4: 'What's this product like with kids and pets?'

What they really want is reassurance.

Customer: 'What's this product like with kids and pets?'

Salesperson: 'Great question, that's such an important thing to think about. Just to let you know, all of our fabric sofas are suitable for heavy domestic use.[10] Who else will be using it at home, and what kids and pets are you referring to? And what colour were you thinking of?'

Each FAQ is an opening. Instead of seeing them as interruptions, treat them as invitations. Every question gives you a chance to demonstrate expertise, build trust and bring the conversation back to the product.

Foundational question categories

To help you build the habit of asking better questions, group them into categories:

- **Terrible questions:** vague, confusing, closed-ended. Avoid them
- **Open questions:** invite the customer to talk freely and reveal details
- **Rapport-building questions:** strengthen trust and connection
- **Million-dollar questions:** the most insightful and powerful ones

We'll have a closer look at the million-dollar questions shortly, but for now, let's look briefly at the others.

Terrible questions

The worst three questions are the following:

- 'Are you OK there?'
- 'Can I help you?'
- 'Do you need any help?'

Do you ever ask those questions? If you do, you'll usually hear 'We're just looking.' It's not the customer's fault – it's the question you asked, which is a closed question. You may also have heard 'Are you OK browsing?' and, 'If you need any help give us a shout.' Both of these are also terrible things to say to a customer because they kill the opportunity for interaction dead.

Swap it for an open, welcoming line: 'Good morning – what brings you in today?,' 'How can I help you?,' 'What can I help you find?,' 'What's on the list today?' All of these are better alternatives because they are open questions.

Open questions

Open questions uncover needs, lifestyle and decision criteria. They start with who, what, where, when, why and how.

Who – 'Who's mainly going to be using this?' 'Who else will be using it day to day?'

What – 'What combination are you looking for?' 'What colour scheme do you have in mind?' 'What have you got at the moment?'

Where – 'Where in the room will this go?' 'Where have you travelled from today?' 'Where does your current one sit at home?'

When – 'When would you ideally like it delivered?' 'When do you need everything in place by?' 'When did you start thinking about changing it?'

Why – A simple way to soften any *why* question is to preface it with: 'If you don't mind me asking…' And then ask your question: 'Why are you changing from your current one?' 'Why does this one stand out to you?' 'Why now – is there a particular reason for the change?'

How – 'How long have you had your current one?' 'How has it worked for you?' 'How would you like to pay?'

Rapport-building questions

Rapport questions turn a polite exchange into a real conversation. They break the ice, show warmth and make customers feel comfortable.

Think of them as social glue. You're simply giving the customer a reason to relax and talk about something familiar:

- 'Where have you travelled from today?'
- 'Do you mind if I ask whether you've bought from us before?'
- 'I noticed your bag or coat – the colour's beautiful. If you don't mind me asking, where did you get it from?'
- If they mention pets: 'Ah, your fur babies – what have you got?'

Once you find a genuine point of connection – location, loyalty, compliment or pets – barriers drop and trust builds naturally.

Target Trust

In the classroom, I often ask salespeople, 'Have you ever been taking an order and suddenly realised you know exactly where the customer lives or works?'

Everyone laughs and nods. It happens all the time – but usually right at the end, when the customer's already at a ten on the buying journey.

The challenge I set them is: what if you could find that connection when the customer is only at a one or two? If you can build that connection early, everything becomes easier.

A perfect example happened to me at a karaoke night. For years, I'd seen the same gentleman at the bar where my friends and I went to sing. He was in his seventies, always stood on his own with a pint, sang a few songs, clapped for ours and we clapped for his – but we never spoke.

One night I said, 'It's John, isn't it?'

'Yes,' he smiled.

'What did you used to do?'

'I was in the Merchant Navy.'

'So was my dad – who for?'

'Manchester Liners.'

'That's who my dad worked for – Ted Hankinson.'

He paused, looked at me, and said quietly, 'Your mum died when you were a kid, didn't she?'

In under twenty-five seconds we'd gone from strangers to sharing something deeply personal – a connection that had been there all along but needed one simple question to unlock it. After that we sat down together, talked for hours, and he's since become a friend. That moment taught me a powerful truth: trust doesn't appear out of thin air. It comes from making the first move, asking the first question and showing genuine interest.

If we open ourselves up to developing stronger relationships with customers, rather than just transacting, we will come across many more of these important moments of personal connection.

You won't always uncover such a striking link as this example, but you will always move closer to a connection. And once you have a connection, trust follows.

We describe this in training as a pyramid of conversation:

- Chit-chat. In everyday life, chit-chat is just politeness. In sales, nothing is done for the sake of it. Chit-chat has a purpose – a light comment about the weather, a car or a sports top. It's how you break the ice and open the door to rapport.
- Rapport/common ground. Move beyond politeness to find something genuine in common. People like people like them. It might be geography, a sport, family or even something small that connects you. This is why we ask, 'where have you travelled

from today?' Most of your customers will be local and you'll often know something about the area they've come from. This is the connection.

- Connection. Once common ground is established, you feel connected. There's an immediate change in the energy and dynamic of the interaction. The customer feels that you have something in common, so they see you as more than just a salesperson. Everything thereafter becomes more meaningful.
- Meaningful. When the conversation moves beyond the surface level, it feels significant. The customer feels understood, and the relationship begins to deepen. These feelings are subconscious, but we all like knowing we have something in common with another person.
- Trust. At the foundation of the pyramid sits trust. With trust in place, customers share openly, buying feels safe and decisions become natural. You'll know you've reached 'trust' when they ask you, 'Which one would you have?' or 'What would you do?'

Another example of how powerful finding a connection can be came from a store manager in Southampton who had undergone our training. He overheard a customer with a Scottish accent and asked, 'Whereabouts in Scotland are you from?' She said, 'Just outside Glasgow.' He said, 'Whereabouts?' She replied, 'Paisley.' He pressed further: 'Which part of Paisley?' She named the area. He said, 'I grew up there. Which road?' And unbelievably, she named the very road he had lived on.

Both of these stories are true, and they show how these serendipitous connections come about when you're genuinely interested, open-hearted and open-minded. They don't happen if you're hiding behind a desk or sticking to a script. They happen when you're present, curious and willing to share something of yourself, too.

You don't always need full trust to make a sale – some customers will buy because they've already made up their mind – but if you want to turn browsers into buyers and move more people from ones and twos to nines and tens, this journey through the levels of conversation is one of the most powerful tools you can use.

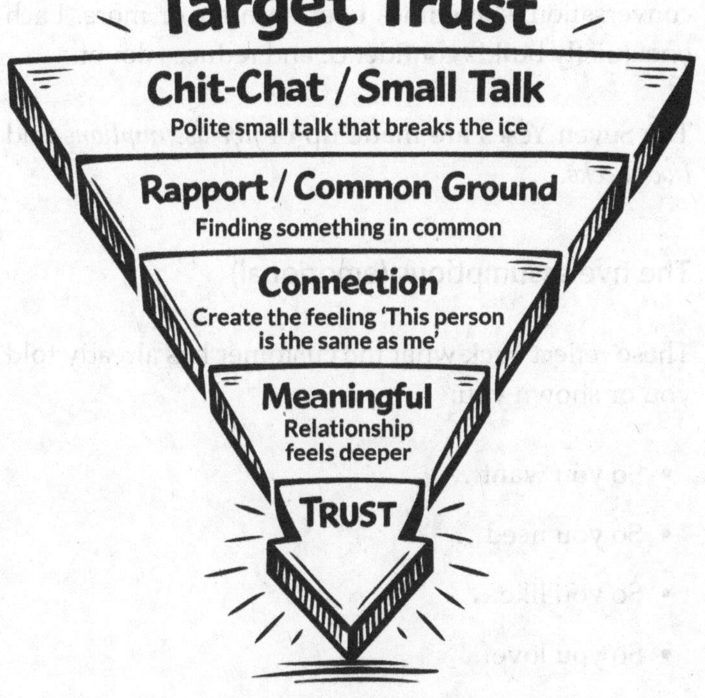

The conversation pyramid

The Seven Yeses

People buy on emotion and justify with logic. That's true whether they're buying a sofa, a bed or a holiday. Very few people make a considered purchase based on one factor alone. They need multiple boxes ticked before they feel comfortable saying yes.

That's what the Seven Yeses are for.

They are not a closing script, and they are not something you run through at the end. They are small moments of agreement that appear naturally throughout the sales conversation, sometimes over an hour or more. Each one quietly builds confidence and reduces doubt.

The Seven Yeses are made up of *five assumptions* and *two checks*.

The five assumptions (emotional)

These reflect back what the customer has already told you or shown you:

- So you want…
- So you need…
- So you like…
- So you love…
- So you're happy with…

These statements confirm the customer's feelings and preferences. They work because they are assumptive. They create momentum and a sense of progress.

For example:

- 'So, it's definitely leather.'
- 'So, you need something durable with the kids.'
- 'So, you love this colour.'
- 'So, you're happy with access on this.'

Each one usually gets a nod or a quiet 'yes.'

The two checks (logical)

These engage the logical part of the brain and confirm understanding:

- Does that make sense?
- Is that right?

They are used whenever you explain something technical, practical or important.

For example:

- 'The backs come off for ease of access. Does that make sense?'
- 'So, durability is the priority over style, is that right?'

These prevent misunderstandings and make the customer feel informed and in control.

Let's put everything together. Here's how a real conversation might sound when you use questions, listening, replaying and assumptive language naturally throughout the customer journey.

Early stage: Opening and discovery

SALESPERSON: 'Good morning, what brings you in today?'

CUSTOMER: 'We're looking for a new sofa. Ours has seen better days.'

SALESPERSON: 'Right, thank you for telling me. What have you got at the moment?'

CUSTOMER: 'It's a three-seater we bought about twelve years ago. It's sagging in the middle and the fabric's worn out.'

SALESPERSON: 'Twelve years, that's a good run. Who mainly uses it at home?'

CUSTOMER: 'Mostly the two of us, but our grandchildren come round at weekends.'

SALESPERSON: 'Got you. So, you need something that'll cope with family visiting too, that makes perfect sense.'

Mid stage: Understanding needs and building the picture

SALESPERSON: 'So what's prompted the change now?'

CUSTOMER: 'It just doesn't feel supportive anymore, and we want something that'll last.'

SALESPERSON: 'So you want something long-lasting, with better support. What sort of look are you drawn to?'

CUSTOMER: 'Something with a higher back, the lower ones don't suit us.'

SALESPERSON: 'So you like the higher back for comfort, that's great. What colours have you got in mind?'

CUSTOMER: 'Something lighter, but not cream, we've got grandkids.'

SALESPERSON: 'So you need a lighter fabric that's still practical for the family.'

CUSTOMER: 'Exactly.'

Later stage: Reassurance and confirmation

SALESPERSON: 'You mentioned earlier you need something durable; this range here uses a fabric called AquaClean. It wipes clean easily and stands up brilliantly to day-to-day use. Does that make sense?'

CUSTOMER: 'Yes, that sounds perfect.'

Salesperson: 'And in terms of size, the four-seater and the two-seater fit your room nicely?'

Customer: 'Yes, that would work perfectly.'

Salesperson: 'So you're happy with the combination, brilliant.'

Customer: 'Yes.'

Salesperson: 'And you said you liked the higher back, this one gives that extra support without feeling bulky. So you're happy with that height?'

Customer: 'Yes, it feels great.'

Final stage: Logical and emotional alignment

Salesperson: 'So we've found something that's comfortable, fits the space and suits your family, does that make sense?'

Customer: 'Yes, it does.'

Salesperson: 'Perfect. So you're happy with the colour, the comfort and the fabric?'

Customer: 'Yes.'

Salesperson: 'Lovely. Let's get this arranged for you.'

Notice how natural the flow feels. Every 'so' builds agreement, every 'does that make sense?' removes doubt, and every replay reminds the customer you were listening. By the time the customer says 'yes' to the order, it isn't a push, it's simply the next logical step in a conversation full of clarity, trust and understanding.

Million-dollar questions

We looked earlier at terrible questions, open questions and rapport-building questions. The final category of question that we still need to explore are the 'million-dollar questions.' We call them this because they lead to million-dollar answers – they don't just open conversations, they uncover what really matters.

Each one earns its place because it moves the sale forward, handles objections early or opens up new opportunities:

- 'What brings you in today?' This gets straight to purpose and can lead straight to the sale.
- 'What have you got at the moment?' This gives you the whole back story of sizes, combination, style, condition, etc.
- 'Why are you changing?' Uncovers motivation.
- 'What are your must-haves?' Prioritises primary buying motives.
- 'Is it leather or fabric you prefer?' Halves the shop instantly.

- 'What size does it need to be?' Handles the 'we need to measure up' objection.
- 'What space are you working with?' Gives context even without measurements.
- 'Apart from yourself, who else is going to be using the furniture?' Finds the real users and a reason to justify five-year protection plans.
- 'Which do you prefer?' An alternate close.
- 'What do you think?' Stops the 'we need to think about it' objection.
- 'What's your timescale?' Less pressure than 'When do you need it?'
- 'Does that make sense?' Checks understanding.
- 'How would you like to pay?' Assumes the order.

Each one of these moves the sale forward and earns better answers.

If you can only remember one million-dollar question, however, make it this one: Drumroll please… **'What's the project?'** This million-dollar question I learned from the top salesperson of a 500-salesperson company – they sold more than anyone else and their average order value was £400 more!

The power of this question comes from the specific wording. As opposed to saying 'What's the situation?' or an alternative question, 'What's the project?' allows the customer to talk about their goals, hopes and dreams much more freely, almost like they weren't a reality.

Allowing them this space to lay out their plans aloud with you means that they're much more likely to open up and tell you things, which would usually take ten times longer.

Ask it early – it shows curiosity and uncovers whole-home opportunities: flooring, curtains, dining, accessories. It's a mindset as much as a question – seeing the customer's bigger picture.

CASE STUDY: The Steve Downey Story

One Saturday morning in Aberdeen, Store Manager Steve Downey, who had recently completed our training, greeted a couple in their forties as they walked into his store.

'Good morning, guys, how are you today?' he said.

'Yeah, we're fine thanks, just come to have a look,' they replied.

Most salespeople would have nodded politely and left them to browse. But Steve didn't. Instead, he smiled and asked, 'What's the project?'

That single question changed everything. The customer explained they were having a large extension built at home – new lounge, dining room and flooring throughout. Instantly, Steve realised this wasn't a casual sofa shopper; this was a potential whole-home project.

He followed up naturally: 'Where are you on your buying journey, one being right at the start and nine being ready to go ahead?'

The man laughed and said, 'Probably about a one and a half.'

It was 10.30 am on a busy Saturday. Most salespeople would have moved on quickly, thinking they didn't have time for a customer 'at one and a half.' But Steve didn't. He stayed with them.

Over the next hour and a half, he asked thoughtful questions, made them coffee, reviewed their plans and showed them flooring, dining tables and sofas. They made notes and took photos but didn't place an order that day.

As they left, Steve walked them out to their car and said, 'Out of interest, where would you say you are now on your journey?'

The man smiled and said, 'Zero on the sofa, couldn't see one we liked, probably a six-and-a-half on the dining furniture, and an eight on the flooring.'

In that moment, Steve knew he'd moved them forward significantly, not just because of the products, but because of the time, questions and genuine interest he'd invested.

The following Saturday, the same couple returned. They placed an order for £18,000 worth of flooring and bought the cabinet furniture through Steve as well, even though they had looked at a store in London.

In total, that couple spent over £30,000 with his store. Why? Because Steve had looked after them. He'd stayed interested and earned their trust. And it all started with one simple question: 'What's the project?'

Most salespeople would have dismissed them at the door. Steve didn't. He gave them time, attention and care and found the bigger opportunity that was there all along.

TIPS, TOOLS, TECHNIQUES, TRY

Tips:

- **Ask before you advise.** The moment you stop telling and start learning, customers feel understood, which is why opening with questions like 'What brings you in today?' work better than launching into product detail.
- **Welcome questions instead of defending.** When a customer asks about sales, pricing or materials, respond positively so they feel safe asking more, rather than feeling shut down or corrected.
- **Soften difficult questions.** Using phrases like 'If you don't mind me asking…' removes pressure and keeps 'why' questions curious rather than confrontational.
- **Build trust early, not at the order form.** Light rapport questions at the start make the rest of the conversation easier because customers open up sooner.
- **Small agreements matter.** Each nod or quiet 'yes' reduces doubt, so confirmation throughout the journey is more powerful than a big close at the end.

Tools:

- **Question categories.** Separating terrible questions, open questions, rapport questions and million-dollar questions helps you choose the right tool for the moment.

- **The Seven Yeses.** Five emotional assumptions and two logical checks give you a simple framework to build agreement naturally over time.
- **Listening and replaying.** Reusing the customer's own words, such as 'want,' 'need,' 'like' or 'love,' proves you've listened and keeps confirmations authentic.
- **The conversation pyramid.** Moving from chit-chat to common ground, then connection and trust, gives structure to what otherwise feels like an informal chat.
- **The buying-journey scale.** Understanding whether a customer is at a one or an eight tells you where they are and what you need to do to move them up. Some people won't buy on the day, but focusing on spending time with every customer, including browsers, will eventually pay off when they become buyers.

Techniques:

- **Assumptive confirmation.** Saying, 'So you need something durable' confirms one of the customer's decisions without pushing, because it reflects what the customer already said.
- **Logical checking.** Using 'Does that make sense?' after explaining access, materials or delivery keeps the customer mentally aligned and reassured.
- **Reframing FAQs as signals.** Treat questions about sales or leather grades as interest, then guide the conversation back to lifestyle and suitability.
- **Rapport through curiosity.** Simple interest in where someone's travelled from or whether they've bought before lowers barriers without feeling forced.
- **Question-led control.** Asking the right follow-up question keeps you leading the journey gently rather than reacting to whatever the customer says next.

Try:

- **Count confirmations, not minutes.** On your next sale, notice how many natural yeses you earn before price is even mentioned.
- **Replace one bad opener today.** Remove 'Are you OK there?' from your vocabulary and start with a genuine open question instead.
- **Use one replay per interaction.** Mirror one key phrase the customer uses and watch how often they nod without thinking.
- **Add one logical check earlier.** Use 'Is that right?' midway through the conversation instead of saving it for the end.
- **Ask 'What's the project?' once per shift.** Even if the customer seems casual, this question often reveals far more than expected.

5
Advanced Questions

Successful customer interactions depend on our ability to identify and address their unique needs and preferences. Building on the foundational questioning techniques introduced in the previous chapter, we're now going to explore advanced questioning techniques. These will help you peel back more layers and reveal the customer's exact wants and needs.

Probing questions

Probing questions go beyond surface-level responses and uncover deeper motivations. They reveal the 'why' behind choices, which is often the difference between an average and a great sales conversation.

Examples include:

- 'What's prompting the change?'
- 'How do you usually use your living room?'
- 'You mentioned comfort is important, what does "comfortable" mean to you?'
- 'What are the must-haves or deal-breakers for you when choosing this piece?'

The secret here is to ask with genuine interest and then be quiet. Don't suggest possible answers, don't fill the silence and don't give them multiple choices. If you tack on 'Are you replacing something or updating your style?' the customer will probably just choose one of those answers, and you'll miss the bigger picture.

One of the easiest and most effective probing prompts is the phrase: 'Tell me a little bit more…'

It works because:

- It's conversational and nonthreatening.
- It encourages the customer to keep talking without feeling interrogated.
- It often leads them to reveal the deeper context – the real reasons behind their choices.

CUSTOMER: 'My husband and I both sit differently, so the sofa we've got doesn't feel comfortable.'

Salesperson: 'Tell me a little bit more about how you both sit?'

Customer: 'Well, my husband always has his feet up on a footstool, and I curl my legs under me.'

In just two lines, the conversation has gone from a vague problem ('doesn't feel comfortable') to a clear picture of how they actually use the sofa. That level of detail is gold for you as a salesperson.

Avoid answering your own questions

One of the biggest dangers when asking questions is giving away the answer inside the question itself. Salespeople often do this without realising. They start with a good question but then add a suggested answer at the end.

The problem? Most customers will just nod and say, 'Yeah, that's right,' even if it isn't. You lose the chance to uncover what really matters.

For example:

- Instead of: 'So one of your priorities is price, isn't it?,' say: 'What would you say your main priorities are?'
- Instead of: 'You're probably looking for something hard-wearing, right?,' say: 'How important is durability for you?'

- Instead of: 'Are you thinking more about comfort than style?,' say: 'Between comfort and style, which matters more to you?'
- Instead of: 'Would you say grey would be your colour choice?,' say: 'What colours are you drawn to?'

Each of the 'wrong' examples provides the customer with the answer, and they simply agree politely. Each one of the 'right' examples keeps the question open and encourages a genuine response.

The golden rule here is simple: ask the question, then stop talking.

Solution-linking questions

Once you've uncovered the customer's needs, the next skill is to connect those needs to solutions. This is where COW – Customer's Own Words – comes in.

People like people like them. When we use the customer's own words, they subconsciously recognise that we're on the same page. It's linked to the skill of paraphrasing, replaying what they said in a way that feels familiar and natural. This creates comfort and trust because the customer hears their own language coming back.

C.O.W.

CUSTOMER'S OWN WORDS

Customer's own words

Examples:

- 'You mentioned durability was key; would a more hard-wearing fabric be a good option for you?'
- 'You told me you've got pets at home; how do you feel about stain-resistant upholstery?'
- 'You said you wanted the room to feel airy; would this neutral palette suit you?'

Using the customer's words is the most powerful way to make your recommendations land. If they say 'snug,' you say 'snug.' If they say 'airy,' you say 'airy.' If the customer says *pouffe* (a fancy name for a footstool), don't correct them and say 'you mean footstool.' If they say 'couch,' call it a couch. Many customers describe a chaise as a 'corner,' even though you and I know it's technically not, but don't correct them. Correcting language breaks rapport; using their words builds it.

Even more powerful is to link back explicitly with a reminder phrase, such as 'Do you remember you said earlier...' or, 'Do you remember you mentioned....' These simple statements take the customer's own words and frame them as the reason for your recommendation.

Examples:

- 'Do you remember you said earlier that your teenagers sprawl all over the sofa? That's why this hard-wearing fabric is a great option.'
- 'Do you remember you mentioned your husband always has his feet up? This chaise end would give him the comfort he's looking for.'
- 'Do you remember you said earlier you curl your legs under when you sit? That's why this deeper seat works better for you.'
- 'Do you remember you mentioned you were matching grey walls? This colour tone will tie in perfectly without making the room too dark.'
- 'Do you remember you said earlier you wanted the room to feel airy? That's why I've suggested this lighter fabric, it keeps the space open.'

These linking statements bring the conversation full circle: the customer hears their own words repeated back as the reason to buy. It doesn't feel like selling, it feels like confirming what they already know is right.

Softening questions

Not every customer will walk into your store relaxed. Some are anxious, uncertain or defensive, especially if it's their first time making a big purchase. Softening questions put them at ease. They reassure customers you're not there to pressure them, but to listen and help.

How do we make questions softer? The answer is tone and language. We calm our voice, maybe drop our volume and use softer, more reassuring words.

With an anxious customer, use the power of tone – calm is contagious. Lower your voice, slow your pace and soften your delivery. This simple shift is transformative. It's the principle of 'calmness is contagious,' a phrase popularised by US Navy SEAL commander Jocko Willink. On the battlefield, panic spreads quickly, but so does calm, a leader who stays measured and quiet steadies the whole team. The same applies in sales. If the customer is flustered and you match their energy with more speed and pressure, you fuel their anxiety. However, if you remain calm, gentle and reassuring, they will mirror you.

Medical research confirms this effect. Studies of surgeons found that those who spoke calmly, warmly and respectfully were sued far less often than those who sounded rushed or dismissive, even when surgical outcomes were identical. Tone shaped trust more than skill. The same is true in our showrooms: tone either builds trust or erodes it.

As well as tone, the language we use can also soften our approach. Asking permission before a question gives the customer control and makes them feel comfortable.

Examples include:

- 'Do you mind if I ask what brings you in today?'
- 'Can I just check whether you were thinking leather or fabric?'
- 'If you don't mind me asking, how were you planning to pay? The only reason I mention it is because we have options like interest-free and low monthly payments available.'

Permission-based questions lower customers' defences and make them far more open. Combined with a calm tone, they turn an interrogation into a conversation.

The 'setting aside' technique

When a customer says, 'We're not buying today,' it does *not* mean you stop selling. It simply means you change *how* you sell. You relax your approach, soften your language and remove pressure. But you should still have every intention, if it's possible, to win the order on the day.

In fact, many customers who say 'We're not buying today' end up doing exactly that. They say it because they want to feel safe, not because they've ruled the purchase out. Handled correctly, it gives you permission to sell properly.

A calm response like, 'That's absolutely fine, it's a big decision, there's no rush and no pressure from us' reassures the customer immediately. The conversation stays alive, and trust builds.

This is where the Setting Aside technique comes in. Rather than challenging the statement or backing away, you gently park the decision and continue the conversation in a relaxed, helpful way. You might say, 'That's no problem at all. Just setting today aside for a moment, when you do come to it, what will be most important to you?'

By pushing the decision into the future, you make it safe for the customer to engage in the present. You can also use the same approach to set aside specific concerns without dismissing them:

- 'Just setting price aside for a moment, what are you really looking for in terms of durability and build quality in this sofa?'

- ‘Putting delivery times to one side, tell me more about how you’ll use the dining table day to day.’
- ‘Ignoring colour choice for a second, what matters most to you in terms of comfort and support in your sofa?’

Each time, you’re not avoiding the issue. You’re simply preventing it from stopping the conversation too early. Customers often repeat ‘We’re not buying today’ several times during a visit. That’s normal. It usually means they’re getting closer, not further away.

Ironically, it’s the lack of pressure that allows many of those customers to buy on the day. They feel understood, comfortable and in control, so the decision becomes easier.

Set it aside softly. Keep selling calmly. Let the customer decide when they’re ready.

Funnel questions

A funnel is simply a way of structuring a conversation so it starts broad and gradually narrows. You begin with open, high-level questions, then layer in more specific ones, guiding the customer step by step towards clarity and, ultimately, a decision.

Some people haven’t heard the term ‘sales funnel’ before, but they instinctively understand how it works. Think of it as the opposite of a 'ladder conversation.' A ladder conversation can move up or down but doesn't really take you anywhere. A funnel conversation, on the other hand, always has direction. Each question narrows the focus and moves you closer to the end of the sale.

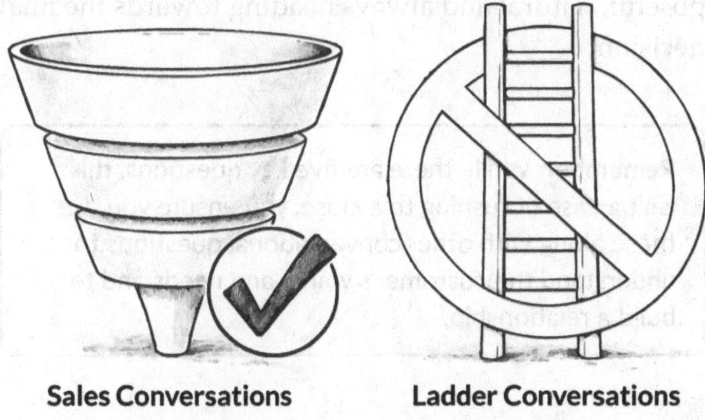

Sales conversations vs ladder conversations

You see this approach everywhere, not just in retail. An estate agent might start with, 'What sort of property are you thinking of?' That broad question could lead to, 'A four-bedroom detached,' which then naturally opens the door to more focused questions about location, budget, garden size and timescales. A holiday consultant might ask, 'Where are you thinking of going?' If the answer is Canada, the conversation immediately narrows into questions about cities, scenery, activities and travel dates.

Furniture sales are no different. Funnel questioning helps you move from general context into meaningful detail without sounding scripted or interrogative. You're not jumping around randomly. You're guiding the customer forward, one layer at a time.

That's why we use it. It keeps the conversation purposeful, natural and always heading towards the final decision.

> **Remember:** While there are five key questions, this isn't a case of rushing to a close, you ensure you use these along with other conversational questions to understand the customer's wants and needs and to build a relationship.

What follows is a clear, practical illustration of exactly how to use the Five-Step Funnel on the shop floor.

Picture this in your mind. Each blank canvas turns into a small scene, moving downward step by step. It's how we move from the big picture to the fine detail:

1. **Empty room:** The first canvas is a completely empty room. The question that belongs here is, 'What room are you doing?' It sets the scene and gives you context straight away.
2. **Teenagers and the dog:** On the second canvas, imagine a teenage boy bouncing a ball on the

floor and wall, while his sister chases an Alsatian around the room. The question here is, 'Who will be using it, and how will they use it?' This is a lifestyle and 'use and abuse' question. The answers tell you about wear, durability and family life, the perfect information to justify things like five-year stain protection later in the sale.

3. **Wallpaper and matches:** On the third canvas, the boy stops bouncing the ball, the girl stops chasing the dog, and she lights a match. The question that goes with this is, 'Are you decorating, or are you matching what you already have?' This question helps you understand whether they're working within existing décor or creating something new.

4. **Match and floor:** On the fourth canvas, the match falls and lands gently on a parquet floor. The question linked to this is, 'What are you doing with the flooring, keeping it or changing it?' This opens up opportunities to talk about flooring, rugs or colours that tie in with existing finishes.

5. **Tape measure:** On the final canvas, the match rolls across the floor, goes out, a small wisp of smoke rises, and it stops dead next to a giant chrome Stanley tape measure. The question here is, 'What space are you working with?' It's better than asking, 'What size do you need?' as it keeps the conversation open and allows you to talk about proportions and layout naturally.

Funnel questions

Each of these five canvases connects an image to a question, and each question moves you one layer deeper into the customer's world. Once you've visualised the pictures, you'll never forget the order of the funnel again.

The funnel doesn't 'erase' when you reach the bottom. You carry all five insights forward into the rest of the conversation. It's a structure that gives you direction without making you sound robotic.

Each step feeds the next, moving naturally from context, to lifestyle, to design, to practical detail, until you have a clear, complete picture of the customer's project.

A good funnel feels like a conversation, not a checklist.

Salesperson: 'What room are you doing?'

Customer: 'We're redoing the lounge.'

Salesperson: 'Lovely, the lounge is such an important room. Is it more for relaxing or entertaining?'

Customer: 'Mainly relaxing, we like watching films together in the evenings.'

Salesperson: 'Perfect, so comfort is going to be really important. Who will be using it, and how often will they use it?'

Customer: 'Mostly us and the kids every day.'

Salesperson: 'Got you, so it needs to work for both adults and children. Teenagers, I'm guessing?'

Customer: 'Yes, fourteen and sixteen, they sprawl everywhere!'

Salesperson: 'Brilliant, so we'll want something durable as well as comfortable. Are you decorating, or are you matching?'

Customer: 'Matching, we've just painted grey.'

Salesperson: 'Nice, grey is so versatile, that gives us plenty of options. What are you doing with the flooring?'

Customer: 'Keeping the oak floor.'

Salesperson: 'Perfect, oak works beautifully with lots of fabrics and colours, so we'll tie in with that. And what space are you working with?'

Customer: 'About five by four metres.'

Salesperson: 'That's a great size; it gives us lots of flexibility. Let's look at what fits best with your doors and windows.'

The funnel provides structure, but the natural back-and-forth keeps it conversational. Think of it like ping-pong: light, rhythmic and engaging, never forced or mechanical.

By the time you've reached the bottom of the funnel, you've gathered everything you need to make confident, tailored recommendations that feel personal to the customer.

Establish needs

Once you've worked through the funnel, you'll already have a clear picture of the room, the users, the layout and the practical details. Now it's time to establish the customer's needs – the essentials that will drive their decision.

Establishing needs is about identifying what matters most to them. It's not just what they want to buy, but why it matters. These are the anchors that will keep your recommendations relevant and powerful.

You can establish needs in two simple ways:

- By asking direct need questions – 'What are the most important things you're looking for?' or, 'What do you need this furniture to do for you?'
- By listening for clues – words like *need, must, important, essential, can't, struggle* or *hate*. Each of those words tells you what they care about most.

Customers sometimes don't even realise what their real needs are until they start talking. Your role is to listen, read between the lines and help them find the words. When they say, 'We just need something comfy,' they might actually mean, 'We're both struggling with back pain.'

Once you've identified their key needs, replay them back for clarity and confirmation:

'So you need something supportive with a higher back, is that right?'

'So you're looking for something practical that's easy to clean?'

This simple reflection confirms understanding, builds trust and proves you're listening. It's also your cue for the next stage: prioritising those needs so you know which ones matter most.

When you move on to priorities, remember: all customers have multiple wants, but only a few real needs. Your job is to uncover the difference.

To start understanding this, simply ask the question 'What do you need this X, Y and Z to do for you?'

Three must-haves

Once you've established the customer's needs, the next step is to help them identify and prioritise what really matters. We call this discovering their Top Five Priorities, and from those, we can uncover their three must-haves, the three things that the product or service *must do* for it to be absolutely right for the customer.

In the classroom, we start by asking salespeople to think of themselves as a customer. 'If you were shopping for a sofa, a bed, a carpet or dining furniture,' we say, 'what would be your Top Five Priorities?' We give them a few minutes to think about it, and they write down their answers, things like style, comfort, price, delivery or access.

Then we take it further. 'OK,' we say, 'now tell me your three must-haves.' At this point, people often pause, rethink and reshuffle their list. It makes them realise how the order changes when they have to choose what really matters.

That same process is exactly what you do with customers. Ask them, 'What would you say are your Top Five Priorities for your new sofa (or bed, dining set or carpet)?' Then follow up with, 'And from those, what would be your three must-haves?'

The answers you get are gold. They give you a clear map of what's driving the decision and what you must get right to earn the sale.

But don't stop there, go one layer deeper. When a customer says, 'Comfort,' ask, 'What do you mean by comfort?'

One person might say, 'It's got to be a foam cushion because I don't want to sink too low, I need support to stand up easily.' Another might say, 'It needs head support but not be too deep front-to-back.' Comfort is subjective, so keep peeling it back until you understand what comfort means to *them*.

If a customer says, 'Price,' ask, 'What do you mean by price?' Almost every time, they'll say, 'I don't mean the cheapest, I mean the best value. I don't mind spending a little more if it's right.' That's a huge opportunity to show value and differentiate yourself from other retailers.

You can use this exercise directly with customers in a simple, natural way:

'What are your three must-haves with this bed?'

'What problems has this sofa got to solve for you?'

'What are your must-haves with this dining set?'

Their answers might be things like, 'It has to seat twelve people for Christmas,' 'It needs to be serviceable for the kids,' or 'It must match a sideboard we already have.' Each response gives you clarity about priorities, and proof that you're listening.

We call this process helping the customer think clearly and feel good. You're not just asking questions; you're helping them organise their own thoughts, set their own priorities and move confidently toward a decision.

By the end of this process, you'll have uncovered the customer's primary buying motives, and that's crucial. It's the difference between guessing what matters and knowing exactly what to present and how to present it.

The reason 'three' is so powerful is simple: one or two ticked boxes rarely create enough certainty for a considered purchase, but three do. There's something about the power of threes; when a customer feels you've met one of their top priorities, then another and then a third, they relax. It just feels right. They may compromise on the other two, but they're delighted that you've met the three things that mattered most. Now that you've discovered their three primary buying motives, your mission is to tick those boxes while the customer is in the store with you. *If a customer leaves without buying we almost certainly didn't establish their three primary buying motives!*

Take a few minutes now to complete the following exercise.

YOUR TOP FIVE PRIORITIES

Excellent customer service starts with understanding our customer's lifestyle, needs and wants. We need to ask great questions and listen to the answers before offering our advice or a possible solution: *'Find out what's important to the customer and make it important to you.'*

If *you* were shopping for sofas what would be *your* Top Five Priorities?

Picture the room

One of the most effective classroom exercises we run is called 'Picture the Room.' It helps salespeople move beyond selling a single item and start understanding the full scope of a customer's project. Most sales conversations begin with an anchor item. A customer says, 'We're looking at sofas today,' and that becomes the sole focus of the conversation. In effect, the salesperson only sees what's directly in front of them. It's like looking into the customer's room through a keyhole. You can see the sofa, but nothing else.

The real opportunity appears when you 'open the door and step into the room.' Picture the Room is about helping the customer describe the entire space, not just the main item they came in for. Who uses the room? Who sits where? What furniture is staying? What's being replaced? What else needs to work together? The conversation always starts with that simple million-dollar question we looked at earlier: 'What's the project?' From there, you build the picture by asking about the room as it exists now, the other furniture within it, the layout and how the space is used day to day. Rugs, tables, lighting, sideboards and accessories often come into view naturally. Many of these are items the business already sells, but they're only uncovered if the salesperson takes time to see beyond the anchor product.

The most effective way to do this is to sit down with the customer and sketch the room together. At a sofa with a coffee table, or at a dining table, a piece of paper comes out and the room is mapped collaboratively. Some retailers even provide graph paper for this purpose. Customers respond extremely well to it. It feels thoughtful, professional and engaging. Instead of feeling like they're being sold to, they feel involved in a joint discovery and co-design process.

This matters because most furniture orders still only contain two or three items. A three-seater and a two-seater, perhaps a protection plan or delivery charge. Yet we know that customers rarely think in single items. Just as someone buying a suit for a wedding also needs a shirt, shoes and tie, or someone buying an outfit also needs accessories, furniture customers often buy the main piece in one place and everything else elsewhere. This isn't because they don't want more, but because nobody helped them see the whole picture.

One company we worked with demonstrated this perfectly. The salesperson began with the question, 'What's the project?' The customer replied, 'We're doing up an Airbnb and we need some single beds.' Rather than stopping there, the salesperson asked a few more questions about how many rooms were involved and what other spaces were being furnished. It quickly became clear this was a much larger job. An appointment was arranged, the customer spent two to three hours in store, and the full project was mapped out. The result was an order of fifty-six items, worth over £13,000. Without those initial questions, the customer would have bought a handful of beds and gone elsewhere for the rest.

The lesson is simple. When you take time to 'Picture the Room,' you improve the quality of the conversation, uncover the full opportunity and deliver a far better experience for the customer. You're not overwhelming them or pushing extra products. You're understanding the project properly and helping them solve it in one place. And, when appropriate, a simple reminder that everything can sit on one interest-free agreement often makes a larger order feel easier to say yes to, turning a single sale into a memorable one.

Room through a keyhole

The Power Of 'What's The Project?'

I want to finish this chapter by being very clear. Of all the questions I've come across in over forty-five years of selling, 'What's the project?' is the single greatest opportunity-creating question I've ever learned. What's interesting is that I only discovered it around ten years ago, on one of our own training courses, when a top-performing salesperson used it naturally and without hesitation.

In Chapter 4, we explored how Store Manager Steve Downey transformed a 'just looking' conversation into a £30,000 sale by asking that one simple question. It was the turning point that revealed a full home extension instead of a single sofa sale. That story captures the core principle, but in advanced sales, 'What's the project?' becomes far more than a question. It becomes a mindset.

The best salespeople use it instinctively to expand every conversation beyond the product in front of them. They don't just want to understand the sofa. They want to understand the room, then the adjoining rooms, the flooring, the lighting and ultimately the lifestyle that connects it all. The moment a customer starts describing their project, the salesperson is mentally mapping the bigger picture, not to upsell, but to see the full scope of what the customer is trying to achieve.

This shift moves you away from thinking in single-sale terms and into whole-home solutions. You begin to recognise natural links. If a customer is changing flooring, rugs may follow. If it's an extension, lighting, dining furniture and accessories are likely part of the plan, too. The driver here is curiosity, not pressure. You're helping the customer think more clearly about what they're doing, and in doing so, you often uncover opportunities they hadn't yet considered themselves.

When you adopt the 'What's the project?' mindset, you stop being just a product expert and become a partner in the customer's world. You help them visualise the complete picture. The room. The home. The feeling they want to create. Then you show them how your business can help deliver it all under one roof.

When we introduce this question to salespeople, many are surprisingly reluctant to use it. Some don't like the sound of the word 'project.' Others feel it's too vague. My advice is simple. Try it. Ask it exactly as it is. Don't dress it up. Don't add 'today' to the end of it. If you ask, 'What's the project today?' you'll often get a narrow answer like, 'We're looking at chairs.' But ask, 'What's the project?' and something different happens. People open up.

If your ambition is to become a million-pound seller, this is where I would start. One question. Asked with genuine curiosity. Repeated habitually. It has the power to turn ordinary conversations into extraordinary opportunities.

TIPS, TOOLS, TECHNIQUES, TRY

Tips:

- **Ask with genuine interest, and then be quiet.** Don't suggest possible answers, don't fill the silence and don't give them multiple choices.
- **Listen for words like 'need,' 'must,' 'important,' 'essential,' 'can't,' 'struggle,' or 'hate.'** Each of these tells you what they care about most.
- **Remember: calm is contagious.** If the customer is flustered and you match their energy, you fuel their anxiety.
- **Never correct the customer's language.** If they say couch, call it a couch. If they say corner, don't say chaise.
- **Don't retreat when you hear 'we're not buying today...'** It's a defence mechanism, not a rejection.

Tools:

- **The Five-Step Funnel** – five blank canvases, one above the other, each representing a layer of understanding.
- **COW (Customer's Own Words)** – replaying the customer's language so they hear their own words coming back.
- **The phrase 'Tell me a little bit more...'** – conversational, non-threatening and encourages deeper context.
- **Permission-based questions** – 'Do you mind if I ask...?' or 'If you don't mind me asking...'
- **The Setting Aside line** – 'Just setting today aside for a moment, when you do come to it, what will be most important to you?'

Techniques:

- **Probing questions** – uncover the 'why' behind choices, not just the surface answer.
- **Avoid answering your own questions** – remove the suggested answer so you don't get polite agreement.
- **Solution-linking** – explicitly connecting needs to recommendations using the customer's words.
- **Softening questions** – calming tone, slower pace and reassuring language to lower defences.
- **Funnel questioning** – starting broad and gradually narrowing so the conversation always has direction.

Try:

- **Use 'What's the project?' exactly as it is.** Don't add 'today' to the end of it.
- **Let a customer finish speaking before you respond.** Silence often reveals the real reason behind the answer.
- **Replay a need back for confirmation.** 'So you need something supportive with a higher back, is that right?'
- **Try the Setting Aside method.** For example, 'Just setting price aside for a moment...' and continue the conversation calmly.
- **Link back before recommending.** 'Do you remember you said earlier...' and let their own words justify the solution.

6
Habit 4: Listening (Active)

You may well be familiar with the proverb that tells us we have two ears and one mouth so that we can listen twice as much as we speak. I once asked Sir Graham Kirkham, the founder of DFS, Britain's biggest furniture retailer with a turnover of over £1 billion, what he believed was the single most important skill of a salesperson. His answer came without hesitation: listening.

I've been married for thirty-five years. My wife loves me dearly, but she often 'coaches' me on my listening skills. And she's right to. This will sound familiar to many couples. In long marriages, and let's be honest, especially in male–female couples, it's usually the man who gets accused of not listening. It's one of the most common domestic frustrations of all.

There's science to back this up. Several studies have shown that men are more prone to 'selective listening' than women, often filtering information based on what they feel is important or relevant to them. In 2019, a nationwide study by Scrivens Hearing Care and OnePoll, published as *The Sound Insight Report 2019: The state of the nation's attitudes to hearing loss,* found that men are almost twice as likely as women to be accused of not listening in relationships.[11] The report revealed that 70% of adults believe their partner has 'selective hearing,' with men significantly more likely to be the culprits. Brain-imaging research also suggests that women may process speech with more areas of the brain engaged simultaneously, whereas men are more likely to focus narrowly, which can appear (and feel) as if they're not listening at all.

That's the heart of it, the feeling of not being heard is one of the most frustrating experiences in any relationship. At home, it causes friction. In sales, it causes customers to switch off, shut down and walk away.

Part of the problem is motivation. We're more likely to listen properly when there's something in it for us. At home, if the conversation feels routine or familiar, we tune out. In sales, if we think a customer is 'just browsing' or even a 'tyre kicker,' we let our attention drift. But when it's a £5,000 comeback, suddenly we're focused, present and alert to every word.

That inconsistency is the real danger. Professional listening means being as sharp and attentive with the customer who appears to be browsing as with the one who clearly has the money to spend. We can never actually know which is which. The quiet, hesitant couple you half-ignore could be about to furnish a whole house. The person you dismiss as a timewaster could be tomorrow's biggest order.

Salespeople who master listening consistently, regardless of first impressions, are the ones who understand their customers' needs faster, build stronger trust and close the bigger sales.

The gap between customers and salespeople

Interestingly, many salespeople believe their biggest weakness is closing. But when customers are asked what salespeople do poorly, their number one complaint is far simpler: they don't listen.

Research by Huthwaite International found that, while 85% of customers expect salespeople to listen carefully, only 39% felt they had actually received adequate attention during their last major purchase, a striking gap that represents a huge opportunity for anyone prepared to listen properly.[12]

Part of the reason this gap exists is that salespeople often overrate their own listening ability.

Communication consultant Tim Londergan put it bluntly in *The 4 Key Listening Habits of Successful Salespeople*: 'Many salespeople overestimate their ability to deploy this key negotiation skill, while also lacking an accurate understanding of the basics of their own listening style.'[13]

A significant factor behind this is 'pseudolistening.' Salespeople nod, maintain eye contact and give all the signals of listening, but in reality, they're mentally preparing their reply, thinking about their pitch or even tuning out entirely. To the salesperson, it feels like listening; to the customer, it feels like being ignored. That mismatch is deadly, because in sales it's not what *you* think you did that counts, it's how the *customer perceives* the experience.

Have you ever asked a customer for their name, which they give you, only to forget it a few moments later? Or asked what combination, size or colour of settee they were interested in, and then had to ask again? That's an example of going through the motions rather than being absolutely focused on that particular customer.

Customers notice. Studies consistently show that perceived listening – how well the customer feels they were listened to – is what builds trust, satisfaction and loyalty. One empirical study in the *Journal of Personal*

Selling & Sales Management found that the listening and empathy of a salesperson have a direct, positive impact on both buyer trust and relationship outcomes.[14] In short, you don't get results for thinking you listened; you get results when the customer feels you did.

Great listening isn't just a technique, it's a mindset and a way of being. It's about engaging every sense, not just your ears. To illustrate what that really looks like, there's an ancient Chinese symbol that captures the art of listening better than any modern sales manual ever could: Ting.

The Ting model of listening

The traditional Chinese character for 'listen,' Ting (聽), is a beautiful reminder of what full listening really means.

It combines five elements:

- Ears, to hear the words
- Eyes, to observe body language
- Heart, to listen with empathy
- Mind, to process meaning
- Respect (the symbol of a king), to give the other person your full attention

Listening is not just hearing. It's engaging every sense, every faculty and every ounce of respect you can give another human being.

What does that look like in practice?

- In a sales conversation, listening with your heart means noticing when a customer says, 'We've just moved house' with a sigh. You don't just hear the words; you feel the emotion underneath. You realise they might be stressed, tired and overwhelmed. That's your cue to slow down, reassure them and make the experience easier. Listening with your mind means piecing that together with what else they've told you. Perhaps they have children, or their budget is stretched. Listening with respect means not rushing them, not pushing your agenda, but giving them the gift of space and full attention.
- In a personal conversation, imagine a friend saying, 'I'm fine,' but their body language is tense, their tone flat and their eyes give them away. Listening with your ears alone might make you move on. Listening with eyes, heart and mind means you pick up the signals, ask gently, 'Are you really fine?' and stay with them in that moment. That kind of listening changes relationships.

When you put all these together – ears, eyes, heart, mind, respect – you move from simply hearing words to making the other person feel truly understood. That's when listening becomes transformational.

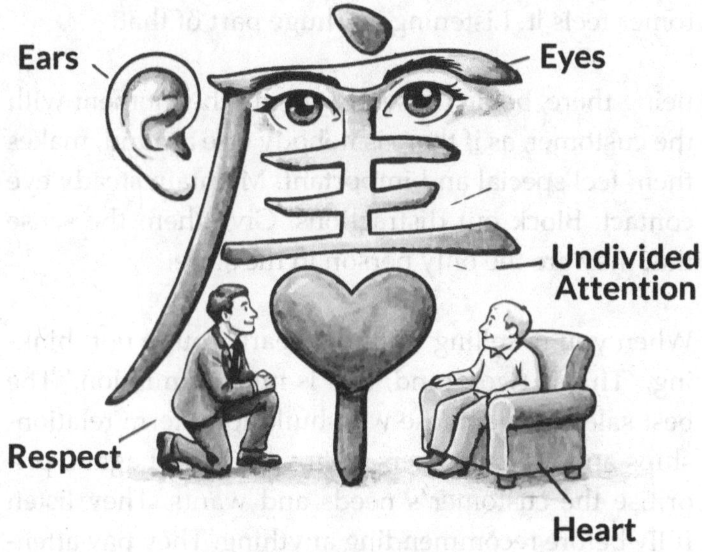

The Ting model of listening

Selling from the heart

This mirrors what Dale Carnegie taught in *How to Win Friends and Influence People*: be genuinely interested in the other person.[15] Customers can spot the difference between someone waiting to make a sale and someone truly curious about their life, their home, their project.

In our own teachings, we describe this as *selling from the heart*; genuinely trying to find the best solution for the customer as a whole, not just what generates the most money today. When you sell from the heart and not from the wallet, it comes across instantly. The customer feels it. Listening is a huge part of that.

Being there, being present, being in the moment with the customer, as if there is nobody else around, makes them feel special and important. Maintain steady eye contact. Block out distractions. Give them the sense that they are the only person in the store.

When you're selling from the heart, you're not thinking, 'This is two grand, this is my commission.' The best salespeople, those who build long-term relationships and see customers return again and again, prioritise the customer's needs and wants. They listen fully before recommending anything. They pay attention to what the customer is concerned about, what they need reassurance about, and what really matters to them, and only then do they suggest solutions.

Customers can sense it. They know when you have their best interests at heart. When they feel that, it's a game-changer. That is authentic, long-term relationship selling, how good listeners become trusted advisers, not just salespeople.

People buy on emotion and justify with logic, and nothing sparks emotion more than being listened to, understood and cared for.

Goldilocks: An incredibly flawed story

Do you consider yourself a good listener?

OK, here's a quick test. Read the following story carefully and then, without looking back, answer the questions that follow. Let's see how you get on.

One day, Goldilocks decided to go for a walk in the forest. Pretty soon, she came upon a house. She knocked on the door, and when no one answered, she walked right in.

At the table in the kitchen, Goldilocks saw three bowls of porridge. Goldilocks was hungry. She tasted some porridge from the first bowl.

'This porridge is too hot!' she exclaimed. So, she tasted the porridge from the second bowl. 'This porridge is too cold!' she said, so she tasted the next bowl of porridge. 'This porridge is just right,' she said happily and tucked into it.

After she'd eaten her fill of porridge, she decided she was feeling a little tired, so she walked into the next room, where she saw some chairs. Goldilocks sat in the first chair to rest her feet.

'This chair is too big!' she exclaimed. So, she sat in the second chair. 'This chair is too big as well!' she whined, so she tried the smallest chair. 'Ah, this chair is just right,' she sighed. But as she settled into it, it broke into tiny pieces.

Goldilocks was very tired by this time, so she went to the bedroom. She lay on the first bed, but it was too hard. She lay on the second bed, but it was too soft. Then she lay on the third bed, and it was just right. Goldilocks fell asleep.

While she was sleeping, the three bears came home.

'Someone's been eating my porridge!' said Papa Bear.

'Someone's been eating my porridge!' said Mama Bear.

'Someone's been eating my porridge, too!' said Baby Bear.

'Someone's been sitting in my chair!' said Papa Bear.

'Someone's been sitting in my chair!' said Mama Bear.

'Someone's been sitting in my chair and broken it all to bits!' said Baby Bear.

The bears decided to look around some more, and when they got to the bedroom, Papa Bear growled:

'Someone's been sleeping in my bed.'

'Someone's been sleeping in my bed, too!' said Mama Bear.

'Someone's been sleeping in my bed, and she's still there!' cried Baby Bear.

Goldilocks woke up, and when she saw the bears, she jumped up and ran out of the room. She ran downstairs, opened the door and ran away into the forest.

Goldilocks listening quiz

Answer Yes or No to each question. You must choose one – if you leave it blank, it's counted as wrong.

1. Was Goldilocks a little girl? □ Yes □ No
2. Did she knock on the door before entering the house? □ Yes □ No
3. Did the bears have porridge for breakfast? □ Yes □ No
4. Was Papa Bear's porridge too hot? □ Yes □ No
5. Were there three bears? □ Yes □ No
6. Did Goldilocks eat all the porridge in one bowl? □ Yes □ No
7. Were there three chairs in the lounge? □ Yes □ No
8. Did Goldilocks break Baby Bear's chair? □ Yes □ No
9. Did Goldilocks go upstairs to the bedroom? □ Yes □ No
10. Was Mama Bear's bed too soft? □ Yes □ No

11. Was Goldilocks frightened when she saw the bears? □ Yes □ No

12. Did she run off into the forest? □ Yes □ No

To check your answers go to https://drive.google.com/file/d/1BL8Ls5c0lGxLGv7Vg9bS8HnhqpKUtpQ9/view?usp=sharing or scan the QR code.

How did you do?

Most people answer quickly and confidently, and many get several wrong. Why? Because they assume. They think they know the story because they've heard it before. They join the dots in their head instead of really, really, really listening to the facts.

That is the whole point of the exercise. It demonstrates how easily we make assumptions. And if we can fall into that trap with a children's story we've known since we were little, how much easier is it to do the same with a customer in our store? Every customer is different. That means every conversation has to start fresh. Forget assumptions. Approach each person with curiosity and an open mind.

Too often, salespeople let their own expectations get in the way. They look at a couple with a toddler and assume they'll only want 'something cheap and practical.' They see a single person on their own and think they're just browsing. They hear 'we're just looking' and take it at face value, instead of hearing the invitation to start a conversation.

But every customer has a story, and unless you uncover it, you can't possibly match them to the right solution.

Starting with a blank canvas

This is a critical concept. When I was selling, I would challenge myself to clear my mind completely before every customer. Whatever had just happened in my last conversation, good, bad or indifferent, I would mentally wipe it clean. I pictured a blank canvas, like those old Etch-a-Sketch toys which you shake and start again. That way, every customer started fresh and every conversation was unique.

The goal was to build a new picture of this customer's world, their situation, challenges, needs and hopes. I wanted to be fully present so the customer felt I was genuinely interested in them and only them.

The very word *conversation* comes from the idea of 'joining me where I live.' That's what it means to really listen and be present. If someone important to you sat down for a meaningful talk, you'd give them your full attention. Customers feel the same way when a salesperson listens like that; they know it's real and they value it deeply.

That discipline changes everything. Too often, salespeople carry assumptions from one interaction into the next, or half-listen because they 'think they know the type.' But when you wipe the slate clean and reset for each customer, you give them your full attention. They feel it. They open up. That's when you get to the truth of what really matters to them.

Being curious is one of the most powerful habits a salesperson can develop. It means asking questions to thoroughly understand the customer, paying attention to what they say, and ensuring you have a complete picture before making any recommendations.

That's how you make the customer feel understood. That's how you avoid assumptions. That's how you turn listening into sales.

Active listening

Listening is not invisible. Customers notice when you're paying attention, and they notice just as quickly when you're not. That's why we call it *active* listening, because it's something you do, not something that just happens.

There are simple behaviours that prove you're actively engaged in the conversation:

- **Nodding:** a gentle nod at the right moment shows you're following along.
- **Eye contact:** maintaining steady yet natural eye contact fosters trust. Research in the *Journal of Nonverbal Behavior* found that appropriate eye contact increases perceptions of honesty, attentiveness and warmth, all vital in building trust.[16]
- **Mirroring and matching:** subtly reflect the customer's pace, tone and body language.
- **Paraphrasing and repeating:** show you've processed and understood.
- **Acknowledgements:** give brief cues like 'I see,' 'That makes sense,' or 'Right.'
- **Body language cues:** give small signals such as tilting your head slightly or leaning forward to show openness and attention.

Finally, the most important signal of all: being fully present. Put the phone away. Don't look over their shoulder. Don't let your eyes dart to the next person walking in. Active listening is giving the customer the respect of your full attention, as though they are the only person in the room.

When customers feel that level of attention, they relax, they open up and they tell you what really matters.

Good listening vs poor listening

Here are common sales scenarios where poor listening loses sales, and good listening wins them.

Scenario 1: A young couple in their first home

Poor listening: The salesperson hears 'we've just moved in' and immediately assumes budget is the only issue. They rush to show the cheapest range.

Good listening: The salesperson asks, 'What kind of space are you trying to create?' The couple explains that they're planning to stay long term and want quality pieces that will last.

Scenario 2: A woman says she wants something practical but stylish

Poor listening: The salesperson hears 'practical' and only shows wipe-clean fabrics.

Good listening: The salesperson asks, 'When you say practical, what do you have in mind?' The customer explains that it needs to stand up to the dog but still look elegant for entertaining.

Scenario 3: A man says he's worried about the kids spilling things on the sofa

Poor listening: The salesperson replies, 'Don't worry, all our fabrics are easy-clean.'

Good listening: The salesperson probes, 'Tell me about your family; how old are the kids?' The man explains they're toddlers who also jump on the furniture. Now, the salesperson knows that both durability and stain resistance are essential.

Scenario 4: An older couple mention back pain and overheating at night

Poor listening: The salesperson hears 'back pain' and only talks about firm mattresses.

Good listening: The salesperson asks, 'How does it affect your sleep?' They learn that the husband overheats easily, so breathability is just as critical as support.

Scenario 5: A customer says they want something simple for their flooring

Poor listening: The salesperson shows the cheapest plain option.

Good listening: The salesperson asks, 'When you say simple, what does that mean to you?' The customer explains they want understated, but with quality that will impress visitors.

Linking listening and the Seven Yeses

You'll remember the Seven Yeses from earlier in the book, the natural confirmations that build momentum and trust throughout the conversation.

The reason they work so powerfully is because they're grounded in listening. You can only use them effectively if you've paid close attention to what the customer has actually said. Each 'yes' is proof that you've heard, understood and respected their words.

When you replay a customer's own language, their *needs, wants* or *loves,* it sends a clear signal: *you were listening*. You wouldn't be able to know which one to say, 'So you need…,' 'So you want…,' or 'So you love…,' without first hearing the customer use those exact words themselves. It's that precision of listening that makes your confirmation feel natural, personal and right.

Without real listening, the Seven Yeses sound mechanical. With it, they feel natural, authentic and human, the subtle rhythm of agreement that turns a good conversation into a great one.

Uncovering black swans

Former FBI negotiator Chris Voss talks about 'black swans,' hidden pieces of information that change everything once they're uncovered.[17] In one of his cases, kidnappers demanded a ransom and negotiators assumed it was all about money. But by listening carefully and probing, his team discovered a hidden truth: the kidnappers were actually fearful for the safety of one of their own relatives. That insight completely changed the dynamic. Instead of treating the ransom as the issue, the FBI addressed the kidnappers' real concern, built trust and de-escalated the situation toward a safe resolution.

A black swan gives you an insight that changes what happens next. It might alter your point of view entirely or simply shift the conversation in a new direction. Either way, you're more likely to reach a positive outcome when you uncover it.

Furniture sales are full of the same principle. A customer might casually ask, 'Is this sofa easy to deliver?' Probe a little, and you might discover they live in a lighthouse with a narrow spiral staircase. Suddenly, from guessing or assuming what the customer might mean when they talk about ease of delivery, you have a full understanding of the real issue and can properly provide the correct resolution.

I once met a customer in her early seventies who had been largely ignored by other salespeople. She mentioned, almost in passing, that she had a hair appointment next door at noon. Most would have taken that as a signal that she was killing time and would be leaving shortly. I didn't. I remember thinking, *She must be here for a reason.*

I asked her the question: 'What's the project?'

She told me she was having a new house built. I said, 'That's exciting.' and asked her to tell me a little more. As she did, she mentioned that she'd already had her flooring measured, but that 'they've lost my selections.' At first, I assumed she meant us, as we sold both flooring and furniture. But by listening carefully and asking one more clarifying question, it became clear she was talking about a competitor. She even named them.

That was the moment everything changed.

I empathised with her frustration and said, 'Look, we offer a free measure as well. There's no obligation and no charge. We've been selling flooring for over 100 years. Why don't you pop back after your haircut and let us take care of it properly?'

She did.

A week later, she placed a £5,300 flooring order with us, around £300 more than the competitor's price. In the weeks that followed, she returned and bought additional furniture for the house as well.

The black swan wasn't the order itself. It was that small, almost throwaway detail: that she had already made flooring selections elsewhere and that the process had gone wrong. If I hadn't listened closely, or if I'd dismissed her because she 'didn't have time,' I would never have spotted the opportunity.

That's the power of careful listening and one well-timed question.

The only way to uncover black swans is to listen – really listen – and then ask the next question. Sometimes a black swan is an unspoken objection, a worry the customer hasn't voiced. When you bring it to the surface and start to tackle the issue, you have the opportunity to earn their trust. Miss it, and you miss the crux of the problem. Catch it, and you give yourself the best chance of winning the sale.

Everyone can relate to this in their own life. In a busy household there's constant chatter and background noise. You filter things out automatically. But then, in an instant, you hear a cry or a scream from your child, and everything changes. You drop what you're doing, run to them, kneel down, look them in the eyes and say, 'What's the matter? What's the matter? What's the matter?' In that moment, you are utterly focused. You're not distracted, thinking ahead or half-listening, you're fully, instinctively present with the most precious thing in your world. That shows the truth of it: there are levels of listening, from passive to truly active. And if your life, or someone you love, depended on it, you'd listen with absolute clarity, intent and heart.

Active listening is not just a courtesy; it's a vital skill. It's the foundation of trust, the gateway to understanding and the beating heart of every successful sale. When you truly listen, with your ears, eyes, heart, mind and undivided attention, you stop making assumptions, uncover black swans, and connect on a level that customers remember. They may forget prices, features or even product names, but they will always remember how you made them feel.

TIPS, TOOLS, TECHNIQUES, TRY

Tips:

- Treat every customer like a buyer until proven otherwise.
- Pause for a full two seconds before replying, it invites them to add more.
- Echo their words. Using phrases like 'cosy,' 'practical,' or 'snug' makes them feel heard.
- Listen with intent, not habit. Notice when your mind starts drifting and bring it back to the customer.
- Always assume there's a black swan, a hidden clue or emotion, waiting to be uncovered.

Tools:

- **The Ting model.** Ears, eyes, heart, mind, full attention.
- **The Goldilocks exercise.** Train yourself to stop assuming you already know.
- **A listening checklist.** After each customer, ask yourself: 'Did I paraphrase?,' 'Did I pause?,' 'Did I summarise?'
- **The Seven Yeses tracker.** Note when you used genuine confirmations that reflected the customer's own words.
- **The Blank Canvas reset.** Mentally wiping the slate clean before every customer so each conversation starts fresh, without assumptions from the last interaction.

Techniques:

- Let the customer do 80% of the talking, especially early on in the process.
- Use summary closes and the Seven Yeses to prove you've been listening.
- Probe for black swans, pick up on throwaway comments and explore them.
- Mirror tone and pace naturally; don't imitate, align.
- Use silence strategically, sometimes the most powerful listening happens when you say nothing.

Try:

- For the next week, treat every customer as though they could be a £5,000 order. Notice how it changes your focus.
- Run the Goldilocks exercise in your next team meeting and see how many assumptions people make.

- After every conversation, write down the three most important things you heard, not what you said.
- Observe colleagues on the shop floor and note when their listening turns from passive to active.
- At the end of each day, reflect: who today felt that I truly listened to them?

7
Habit 5: Selling The Solution

Isn't it interesting that we're now over halfway through the book and haven't yet begun to discuss selling? The same is true of our award-winning two-day course: it isn't until well past mid-morning on day two that we get into this stage.

Why? Because so much has to happen before you can sell anything. You need the right mindset, the right approach, the right questions and the right listening skills. Too many salespeople skip this and rush straight to downloading product information at the customer. It's precisely the wrong way round.

By the time you reach this point, you've already asked tremendous questions: 'What's the project?' 'What are your must-haves?' 'What do you like and not like?' 'Tell me about your lifestyle.' You've done a full discovery. Now you know what's relevant, what's important and what matters most to this customer. In real life, you would have already been gently guiding and narrowing choices; for teaching purposes, we're drawing a clearer line.

Think of it as opening them up before closing them down: start wide, let them explore, then gradually narrow to the best fits. You're no longer shooting in the dark, you're recommending with focus and clarity.

Knowing enough

Confidence is a salesperson's best friend; the greatest source of confidence is through product knowledge. The best way to build that confidence is by learning the essentials first, the best-selling products in your store and the everyday questions customers are going to ask. Things like combination options, fabric choices, lead times, guarantees, cushion filling options and basic durability. Once you can answer those fluently, you'll sound credible and reassure customers they're in safe hands.

When people are brand new to selling furniture, they often think they need to know everything about every product. That's impossible, especially in a business with hundreds of ranges.

Let's talk about the most common FAQs you're going to need to know as a salesperson. These will vary slightly by department, but they tend to follow a similar pattern.

Sofas:

- What combinations are available?
- What fabric, leather and colour options are available?
- What different feet or leg options are available?
- Who is the manufacturer?
- What is the lead time for delivery?
- How is the frame constructed?
- What guarantees and warranties come with it?

Beds:

- What sizes are available?
- What's the difference between the mattresses, and not just the number of springs?
- What storage or base options are available (eg ottoman, divan, drawer)?
- What is the lead time?
- What are the manufacturer's and store guarantees?

Dining and bedroom furniture:

- What sizes and items are included within the range?
- What finishes, colours or handles are
- available?
- What is the lead time?
- What are the manufacturer's and store guarantees?

Find the commonalities across departments and treat this as your foundation knowledge; here's an example of some of the things you should learn first.

We suggest that you learn the most popular selling ranges first, and often it's easier to do that by manufacturer, because many of the features, benefits and product details transfer across their ranges. There's little point in learning a complex, slow-selling product when you're just starting out if it only sells every few months. Instead, focus on the ones you'll be selling three or four times a week and learn those thoroughly. You'll quickly see patterns and similarities that make it easier to build confidence. For example, start with popular manufacturers like White Meadow, Alstons, Harrison Spinks, G Plan or Tempur. You'll soon identify which are the best-sellers in your own store, and if you move on to another department, learn those key manufacturers and their ranges first.

Customer FAQs in practice

One of the fastest ways to build real product confidence is to practise answering the questions customers actually ask. Rather than relying on experience alone and waiting for knowledge to build over months or even years, the most effective teams use FAQs as a structured learning tool.

Take a product range, a manufacturer or a best-selling model and identify the most common questions customers ask about it on the shop floor. New starters and experienced salespeople alike should practise answering those questions with a colleague before they ever face them in a live conversation. This turns product knowledge from something theoretical into something usable.

For example, if a salesperson is learning a new Alstons range, you don't just tell them to 'read the brochure.' Instead, you say: 'These are the questions you're going to be asked.' After a day, a week or however long is appropriate, you test them. Over time, this approach means they quickly learn the key information on your most important products, not by chance, but by design.

Used properly, listing and practising customer FAQs allows you to fast-track learning. One manufacturer this week. Another next week. Instead of only learning answers when a customer happens to ask the question, you build confidence deliberately and consistently.

Below are examples of how common FAQs sound on the shop floor, and how a good salesperson turns each answer from a dry fact into a relevant solution.

CUSTOMER: 'What combinations does this sofa come in?'

SALESPERSON: 'This model comes as a two-seater, three-seater, corner group and even a sofa-bed, so you can pick the layout that works best for your room and how you live.'

CUSTOMER: 'Does it come apart for access?'

SALESPERSON: 'Yes, the arms and backs detach, which means we can guarantee access through standard doorways, so you don't need to worry about it fitting in.'

CUSTOMER: 'What colours and fabrics are available?'

SALESPERSON: 'You can choose from over thirty fabrics, including the AquaClean range you mentioned earlier, which is perfect for pets. That way you get the look you want with the durability you need.'

CUSTOMER: 'How long does delivery take?'

SALESPERSON: 'This range is made in the UK and usually delivered in about eight weeks, so you'll have it in time for Christmas, which you said was important.'

CUSTOMER: 'What's the guarantee?'

SALESPERSON: 'This manufacturer gives a ten-year frame guarantee, which gives you peace of mind that the structure is built to last.'

CUSTOMER: 'What sizes do the beds come in?'

SALESPERSON: 'This range is available in single, double, king and superking, so you can match the right size to your room. You mentioned storage was important, so I'd recommend looking at the ottoman option as well.'

CUSTOMER: 'What's the difference between these mattresses?'

SALESPERSON: 'This one has 2,000 pocket springs, which spread weight evenly, while this one has memory foam that moulds to your body. You said you wanted good support for your back, so the pocket spring would give you that consistent support all night.'

CUSTOMER: 'Does the dining table extend?'

SALESPERSON: 'Yes, it extends from six to eight places, which is great for you because you said you like having family round at weekends.'

CUSTOMER: 'Can we get matching chairs or a bench?'

SALESPERSON: 'Yes, this comes with a choice of chairs or a bench seat. A bench works really well with children because you can fit them side by side more easily.'

CUSTOMER: 'What's this like with pets?'

SALESPERSON: 'You mentioned your two Labradors. This fabric has a tight weave and is stain-resistant, which means it's far less likely to snag, and it wipes clean, so you can keep it looking fresh.'

Here is the Product Champion PDF that we use to help salespeople master their product knowledge. Each salesperson should use one form to research a particular manufacturer and when they feel sufficiently confident, present their findings to their manager and/or team. This is particularly helpful for salespeople who are new to the industry, when you have a new supplier's products on display and where an expert's knowledge can help team members who aren't as confident or knowledgeable. Start using this straight away and your confidence will transfer to customers, creating more sales.

I asked a seventeen-year-old apprentice sales assistant to use this to learn all about Ercol – within one month she had sold a £10,000 order!

To access the Product Champion PDF go to https://drive.google.com/file/d/1by0DIxz6EWNhvIWUng8HT84KyxWxJkoA/view?usp=drive_link or scan the QR code.

Use it to deepen your knowledge and expand the stories you can tell.

Features, benefits and the bridge

We're going to play a bit of a game, and you can do this in your store. We call it the Feature and Benefit Game. For the sake of this exercise, we are going to classify a feature as a fact. In other words, a feature is something that's a cold, hard, provable piece of information.

For example:

- This is a recliner.
- This is two metres long.
- This has got 2,000 springs.

That's what we mean by a feature in this case.

Now we add the three other parts that turn product knowledge into persuasion: benefit, advantage and the bridge.

- **Benefit** is what that feature does for the customer. It's the outcome or improvement they'll feel or experience:
  - 2,000 springs = specific joint and muscle support and comfort.

- Hardwood frame = lasts for years with three kids.
- Recliner mechanism = relax at the touch of a button.
- Bolt-on arms = guaranteed access through tight doorways.

- **Advantage** is what that feature (and its benefit) does compared to another option. This is the 'over the other one you looked at' piece. It answers the unspoken question: why this one rather than that one? For example: 'The advantage of this over that one is…' or, 'Where this really stands out is…' or, 'What makes this different from the others is…'

The bridge is the conversational link that makes the connection clear and personal. It joins the logical fact to the emotional reason to buy. It's the gear that moves the customer between the feature, advantage and benefit. Phrases like:

- '…which is good for you because…'
- '…which is great for you because…'
- '…which is fantastic for you because…'
- '…which is perfect for you because…'

So the full flow looks like this:

- Feature = fact
- Bridge = connection ('good for you because…')
- Advantage = evidence and comparison ('the advantage over that one is…')

Benefit = emotion and outcome (how it will feel or what it will solve)

The Feature and Benefit Game

Here's how you can bring this to life as a game:

1. Pick a product as a group. It could be a sofa, a bed or a dining set.
2. Take 10–15 minutes to list as many features as you can. Aim for at least twenty-five. Remember, features are the cold, hard, provable facts.
3. List the benefits. For each feature, come up with at least one benefit, ideally more, because most features can link to multiple benefits depending on the customer.
4. Add your bridges. Make the connections customer specific. Use 'good for you,' 'great for you,' 'fantastic for you,' and 'perfect for you,' to escalate the emotive impact.

5. Role play. Deliver as many features and benefits as possible in three minutes, as though you're in a real sales conversation.

Extra points are awarded for:

- Using the customer's name
- Charm and charisma
- Making it flow naturally, like a conversation rather than a list
- Linking the features and benefits back to what the customer has already said matters to them

Here's an example of how this should sound:

> 'What I really like about this product, Adam, is that it has what we call a double-sprung seat base, which is great for you because you mentioned wanting both comfort and long-lasting support. The benefit is that these pocket springs spread your weight evenly, so whether you're sitting upright or stretched out towards the TV, it feels consistently comfortable. Does that make sense?'

Delivered this way, you're not just rattling off a list of features. You're demonstrating that you've listened, understood and tailored the product to the customer's needs, while keeping the energy and connection of a real sales conversation.

The psychology behind feature, bridge, advantage and benefit

Most salespeople know the sequence: feature, bridge, advantage, benefit. But few understand the psychology behind it, or why the bridge is the key that turns information into influence. Let's break it down properly.

Feature: The logic

A feature is what something *is*. It satisfies the rational part of the brain, the bit that wants facts.

'The frame is solid hardwood.'

'The cushions are pocket sprung.'

'It comes with a ten-year guarantee.'

That's useful information, but it's not persuasive. At this stage, the customer's brain simply records the data, it doesn't feel anything.

Bridge: The connection

The bridge is where the persuasion begins. It shifts the focus from the product to the person. The bridge is the gear that moves the customer between the features, advantages and benefits. Miss it out, and you're just listing features. Use it properly, and you create belief. That's where great furniture sales happen.

Phrases like:

'...which is good for you because...'

'...which is great for you because...'

'...which is fantastic for you because...'

'...which is perfect for you because...'

These aren't filler lines; they're psychological triggers. They activate the *self-referencing effect*, the moment the customer starts thinking, *me, my home, my comfort*. That small shift transforms logic into relevance. The bridge also reduces effort. You're doing the thinking for them, connecting the dots so they can easily picture the result.

Advantage: The evidence

The advantage gives credibility. It answers the unspoken question: 'So what does that actually do?'

'It won't twist, creak or weaken over time.'

'Each cushion supports you individually, so it never dips or sags.'

'You're completely covered if anything goes wrong.'

The advantage reassures the logical brain. It builds trust that the product performs as promised, and that you know your stuff.

Benefit: The emotion

This is where buying decisions are made. The benefit links everything back to how the customer will *feel*.

'So you'll enjoy that same solid, reassuring comfort every time you sit down.'

'So you'll always have that new-sofa comfort, year after year.'

'So you can relax, enjoy it and know your investment's protected.'

This lights up the brain's emotional centre, the part that drives decisions. People don't buy what the furniture *is*; they buy what it *means*: comfort, pride and peace of mind.

The psychology of the bridge

The bridge is where information becomes influence. When you say, 'which is good for you because...,' you're doing three powerful things at once:

1. You make it personal. Using 'you' puts the customer at the centre of the sentence. It's no longer about a product; it's about *their* life, *their* home, *their* comfort.

2. You make it emotive. Words like *good, great, fantastic,* and *perfect* awaken the customer's feelings, helping them imagine what ownership will feel like.

3. You make it logical. The word *because* gives the reason why, justifies the emotion and provides reassurance.

I'll say it again: people buy on emotion and justify with logic. The bridge connects both sides of the brain: it moves the customer from *feeling* to *reasoning* without friction.

When you build your conversation this way, each recommendation appeals to both the heart and the head. The 'good for you' phrasing creates empathy and imagination; 'because' creates confidence and logic. Used together, they form one seamless sentence that feels natural and persuasive: 'This fabric is from the AquaClean range, which is fantastic for you because you mentioned your two Labradors, so paw marks and spills just wipe off.'

The psychology of 'because'

The power of 'because' was famously proven in a Harvard study by psychologist Ellen Langer. In two different office blocks in America, people queued to use a photocopier. When someone asked, 'Can I use the photocopier?,' about 60% of people let them go through. When they said, 'Can I use the photocopier because I'm in a rush?,' over 90% let them through.[18]

Even more interestingly, when the request was, 'Can I use the photocopier because I need to make copies?,' a weak reason, since everyone needed to make copies, compliance still jumped dramatically. The lesson? People are much more likely to agree when you give them a reason, even if the reason isn't very convincing.

That's why 'because' is so powerful in selling. It transforms a flat fact into a compelling justification, making your recommendation feel logical, credible and emotionally resonant.

Here's an example: 'This sofa is eight feet long, which will be great for you because you said you host Sunday dinners. The benefit is that everyone will be able to fit on it without dragging extra chairs in.'

The simple addition of 'because' turns product knowledge into persuasion. It helps the customer rationalise their emotional decision and feel entirely justified in buying.

Let's have a look at some more examples so you can really see it in action.

Ten worked examples

Sofas

1. **Feature:** 'This sofa has bolt-on arms...' **Bridge:** 'which is great for you because you said access is tight into your lounge...' **Benefit:** 'so we can guarantee it will fit through the door and be built in the room.'
2. **Feature:** 'This sofa is upholstered in AquaClean fabric...' **Bridge:** 'which is fantastic for you because you mentioned your two Labradors...' **Benefit:** 'so spills and paw marks wipe off easily, and you keep it looking good.'
3. **Feature:** 'This sofa comes with a ten-year frame guarantee...' **Bridge:** 'which is perfect for you because you said you're furnishing your forever home...' **Benefit:** 'so you'll have complete peace of mind that it's built to last.'

4. **Feature:** 'This corner group is over eight feet long...' **Bridge:** 'which is great for you because you host Sunday dinners...' **Benefit:** 'so everyone can sit together comfortably without dragging in extra chairs.'

Beds

5. **Feature:** 'This mattress has 2,000 pocket springs…' **Bridge:** 'which is good for you because you said back support is really important…' **Benefit:** 'so your weight is spread evenly and you wake up refreshed.'

6. **Feature:** 'This bed base is an ottoman style…' **Bridge:** 'which is fantastic for you because you said storage space is limited in your bedroom...' **Benefit:** 'so you can store away bedding, shoes or winter clothes without clutter.'

7. **Feature:** 'This mattress has a memory foam layer...' **Bridge:** 'which is great for you because you said you often wake up with sore joints...' **Benefit:** 'so the foam moulds to your body and relieves pressure where you need it most.'

Dining

8. **Feature:** 'This dining table extends from six to eight places...' **Bridge:** 'which is perfect for you because you said you have family around most

weekends...' **Benefit:** 'so you can fit everyone in comfortably without squeezing.'

9. **Feature:** 'This set comes with a choice of chairs or a bench...' **Bridge:** 'which is great for you because you said you've got three young children...' **Benefit:** 'so you can seat them side by side more easily at mealtimes.'

10. **Feature:** 'This dining table is finished with a ceramic top...' **Bridge:** 'which is fantastic for you because you said you didn't want to worry about heat or scratches...' **Benefit:** 'so hot dishes or everyday wear and tear won't damage the surface.'

Taking advantage

Now you've mastered the basic feature–bridge–benefit flow, let's look at a few examples that add the advantage, the 'so what' that compares one option with another and strengthens your recommendation.

You can introduce it naturally with phrases like:

- 'The advantage of this over that one is…'
- 'Where this really stands out is…'
- 'What makes this different from the others is…'

Here are two examples:

1. **Feature:** 'This model has high-resilience foam seat cushions...' **Bridge:** 'which is great for you because you said you wanted lasting comfort.' **Advantage:** 'The advantage over foam-filled seats versus fibre is that the foam cushions will retain their shape even with daily use and very little maintenance except rotating...' **Benefit:** 'so you'll enjoy that same level of support and bounce year after year.'
2. **Feature:** 'This mattress has 4,000 pocket springs with a layer of natural wool...' **Bridge:** 'which is perfect for you because you said you tend to get warm at night.' **Advantage:** 'The advantage over synthetic-filled models is that natural wool helps regulate body temperature and wick away heat...' **Benefit:** 'so you'll stay cool and comfortable in summer, and snug through the winter.'

Adding this extra layer elevates your presentation from simply matching needs to differentiating choices, proving why your recommendation truly is the best fit for them.

Training page layout

In workshops, we present this as a page with four columns to make it practical and straightforward:

Feature	Bridge	Advantage	Benefit
This sofa has bolt-on arms	which is great for you because you said access into your lounge is tight	the advantage over fixed-arm sofas is that it can be brought in in sections, so there's no risk of it getting stuck or damaged during delivery	so we can guarantee it will fit through the door and be built in the room
This mattress has 2,000 pocket springs	which is good for you because you said back support is really important	the advantage over open-coil or fewer-spring mattresses is that each spring works independently, so your body is supported evenly rather than being pushed up in a few pressure points	so your weight is spread evenly, and you wake up refreshed

And so on.

Using this table, salespeople can practise building out their own examples, filling the columns with the features, bridges and benefits for whichever product they're working on.

Feature	Bridge	Advantage	Benefit

The danger of downloading

One of the biggest traps salespeople fall into is what we call 'downloading.' This is when they stand in front of a product and dump every bit of product knowledge they can remember onto the customer.

To the salesperson, it feels impressive. To the customer, it feels overwhelming. It's like trying to drink from a fire hose.

A common version of this happens when a customer is looking at a sofa, and the salesperson goes in with what they think is a 'gift.' They say, 'Oh, just to let you know, this sofa comes in all of these fabrics,' and pull out a rack of twelve swatches. What they think is helpful actually overwhelms the customer. Very quickly, the customer starts asking, 'What's the difference in price? Why are some more expensive? What are the different qualities?' Before you know it, the salesperson has spent an hour explaining fabrics, and the customer leaves saying, 'I can't make a decision today, I'll have to go away and think about it,' or, 'Can you send me a dozen swatches in the post?'

This stems from two sources: a lack of awareness and a personality type that seeks to please. It comes from a 'well of kindness' mentality, and the salesperson thinks they are being helpful, but in reality, most customers facing that many choices are paralysed. They don't buy because they can't process it all.

The better approach is to keep it specific and relevant. For example, go in with a 'gift' by saying: 'Just to let you know, we do this particular model in other colours. What colour did you have in mind?' If the customer says grey, all you need to do is pull out the swatch that shows the grey options within that fabric range. Now you're only dealing with the greys in that one swatch book, not twelve different collections. That keeps the conversation tight, relevant to the buying signal, and easy for the customer to process.

This applies in other situations, too. Salespeople often come back from a factory tour full of technical knowledge and want to share it all. A customer recently told me they'd been in another store where the salesperson spent half an hour 'downloading' everything they knew about Duresta, a high-end manufacturer. The customer wasn't impressed. In fact, they said, 'I'm not interested, I know all about Duresta. I just want to know if it's comfortable and if it comes in the right colour.' That download put them off, and they ended up buying from the salesperson who kept it simple, relevant and customer focused.

Your company's USPs: Blow your own trumpet!

Every business has a story. Customers rarely know it, and salespeople often forget it. DFS began above a disused snooker hall and today, not only sells but also manufactures, with three of its own factories. Oak Furnitureland started with a single person selling pine furniture on eBay and now operates multiple locations. IKEA grew into a global brand from a mail-order venture started by one man. Whether you're part of a national chain or a long-established local store, every business has its roots and a reason it exists today.

That heritage isn't trivial. It's trust. When you tell customers about it, they get a sense that your business is solid, reliable and here for the long term.

Imagine a company that's been established for 100 years in the same town, still family-run, with everything done in-house. That story doesn't just fill a website's 'About Us' page. It builds confidence in every single conversation.

Here are some worked examples of how USPs can be turned into features, bridges and benefits, and why it works for a 100-year-old family business:

Feature: We've been in business for over 100 years...

- **Bridge:** ...which is great for you because...
- **Advantage:** The advantage of using us, compared to buying online or from a newer retailer, is reassurance through experience. We've been doing this long enough to understand every product, every situation and how to handle things properly if anything unexpected crops up.
- **Benefit:** ...so you can feel completely at ease and buy with total peace of mind, knowing you're dealing with experts who will look after you properly at every stage, before, during and after the sale.
- **Why it works:** Longevity signals safety and continuity.

Feature: We're still a family-run business...

- **Bridge:** ...which is great for you because...
- **Advantage:** The advantage for you is the level of care and attention that comes with that. The owners are in the business day in, day out, seeing and hearing every part of the customer experience, so standards stay high and nothing slips through the cracks.
- **Benefit:** ...so you can feel completely comfortable and confident, knowing there's always someone

personally invested in making sure everything is right for you, from the moment you walk in to long after delivery.

- **Why it works:** Customers sense accountability and personal pride.

Feature: We do everything under one roof, furniture, flooring, beds and home accessories…

- **Bridge:** …which is great for you because…
- **Advantage:** The advantage for you is convenience and simplicity. We can plan everything together properly, coordinate it all and even fit the flooring and deliver your furniture on the same day if needed.
- **Benefit:** …so you save time, avoid running around different shops, and have the reassurance that everything will work together smoothly first time.
- **Why it works:** Customers value ease and certainty. Reducing effort, time and coordination removes friction from the buying decision and makes a larger purchase feel manageable and stress-free.

Here are some more hard facts, try coming up with the Feature, Bridge, Advantage, Benefit and Why it works for each.

Team exercise

Grab a notepad and create a four-column table titled 'Your company's USPs: Blow your own trumpet!' The column headings should be Feature, Bridge, Benefit and Why it works. Place one or two of the examples above at the top as a guide. Leave the rest of the page blank for the team to complete during training.

Working as a group, create ten of your own USPs that highlight what makes your store special, whether it's local reputation, specialist services or community connections. This way, every salesperson builds a toolkit of ready-to-use stories they can weave naturally into their conversations with customers.

The key to remember is this: customers who are new to you won't know that story. Returning customers may already come back for those reasons, but when you're inside the business, you can become desensitised to, or take for granted, the vast benefits you have.

That's why it's vital to blow your own trumpet and share them. Pride and passion sell, and you should never hold back or apologise for being passionate about the business you work for. That passion makes you stand out from the competition, whether customers have visited them before or will visit them after. The difference your passion creates will show.

Storytelling in action

Stories are sticky. People tend to forget lists of facts, but they often remember stories. If you want your USPs to land, wrap them in a story:

> 'I understand you're comparing us with others, that makes sense. The key difference is that we've been here for seventy-five years, and our own team handles everything. Our family name is still above the door, and most new customers come from recommendations. People wouldn't send friends and family unless we truly delivered.'

I once went to a restaurant, and a young waitress came over to tell us about the specials. She read through the list, but when she got to one dish, she added, 'We also have organic shoulder of lamb that has grazed in the valleys of the Forest of Bowland.' That single line painted such a picture in my mind that I ordered it, and it was fantastic.

That's the power of storytelling. It doesn't just describe; it paints an image, creates a feeling and justifies value.

In furniture, storytelling is particularly helpful when you're justifying quality or price:

- Vispring began with an engineer making a mattress for his wife in 1899. Over 120 years later, they still handcraft every mattress in Plymouth, with individually pocketed springs and bespoke finishes. When you say, 'This is a Vispring mattress,' you're selling heritage and precision, not just a bed.

- Harrison Spinks grows many of its own natural fillings – wool, hemp, flax – on its Yorkshire farm. Their mattresses are hand-stitched, glue-free and made from British steel springs forged on site. When you tell a customer that their mattress is grown and produced within a few miles of the factory, price fades behind provenance.
- Stressless was born in Norway in 1971, engineered so that the chair moves with the body. Their patented Glide™ and Plus™ systems enable the recliner to adjust seamlessly to your posture. When a customer leans back and feels that motion, the story is simple: decades of Scandinavian design and engineering went into that effortless moment.

This ability to bring products to life with fabulous stories makes customers see and feel the difference. It justifies price, explains value and creates confidence.

Avoiding and handling objections

Before a customer can ever feel ready to buy, they need to feel completely confident in the solution itself.

They need clarity about size, comfort, fabric, delivery, durability and value. The job at this stage is to remove doubt, not create more of it. Many salespeople talk through the product but forget to talk through the customer's doubts. Selling the solution properly means clearing away anything that might hold them back so the decision becomes easy and natural. That's why avoiding, handling and overcoming objections is such an important part of this habit. It's not closing. It's the work that earns the close.

Avoiding objections

Avoiding objections is always better than handling them. If you know what the likely hesitation will be, you can deal with it calmly and naturally before the customer ever feels the need to raise it.

Avoiding objections: Size

In furniture sales, the most common objection isn't price. It's size.

'We need to measure up' is what customers often say when they're unsure, cautious or simply buying time. The mistake most salespeople make is waiting for that objection to appear at the end of the conversation, and then trying to overcome it when the customer is already looking for an exit.

The better approach is to remove the need for the objection altogether by handling size naturally and early. There are three proven ways to do it.

Establish what they have now. Before the customer can say 'we need to measure up,' you establish what they've already got.

On upholstery, one of your earliest questions should be, 'What have you got at the minute?' Most customers will answer with something like, 'A three-seater and a two-seater.' You then follow immediately with, 'Is it the same again?'

If the answer is yes, the size issue is effectively put to bed. Most three-seaters sit between roughly 200 and 220 centimetres, and across most manufacturers the proportions are very similar. If what they have now fits, what they're replacing it with almost certainly will, too.

At that point, there's no new complexity. You've quietly removed the need to 'go home and measure' because nothing fundamental is changing.

Use the room set and ask, 'What space are we working with?' A more relaxed conversational way to handle size is to ask: 'What space are we working with?'

As you ask it, gesture naturally to the room set you're standing in. Most stores display a typical setup: a three-seater, a two-seater, perhaps a chair, plus a coffee table and lamp table. That setting is usually designed to represent an average room, often around four by five metres.

By anchoring the conversation to a visible, real-world reference, you help the customer judge scale instinctively. Most people will say something like, 'About this size,' or 'Slightly bigger than this.'

Again, you've handled size without forcing a measuring trip.

When they ask 'What size is it?' use Russ's question. The third and final way to avoid objections about size is to ask Russ Platt's question. When the customer asks 'What size is it?,' most salespeople answer by quoting dimensions. That often triggers the customer to retreat into, 'We need to measure up.'

Instead, Russ's million-pound answer is: 'What size does it need to be?'

If a customer is asking about size, they often already know the space they're working with. Asked this way, they'll usually reply with something like: 'I've got about 220,' or 'We've got roughly 250 to play with.'

Now you're working with their numbers, not yours. You're no longer guessing, and you haven't created a reason for them to leave the store to check.

Avoiding objections: Price

Price anxiety often sits quietly in the background, even when customers haven't mentioned it. A great salesperson in an interest-free store used to greet every customer with a simple line: 'Just to let you know folks, you can buy anything in here for £20 a week.' Nothing else. No explanation. No pressure.

That one sentence reframed the entire showroom. Affordability was assumed. The customer no longer had to ask, 'Can we afford this?' because the answer had already been given.

Handled early and casually, the price objection often never appears.

Avoiding objections: Durability and lifestyle concerns

Another common hesitation, especially with upholstery, is durability. Customers worry about kids, pets and everyday wear, even if they don't say it outright.

A simple pre-handling line is often all that's needed: 'Just to let you know, all of our fabrics are suitable for everyday domestic use.'

That single sentence answers several unasked questions at once:

- Will it last?
- Is it practical?
- Am I going to regret this?

You haven't turned durability into a problem. You've quietly removed it as a concern.

Avoiding objections: Russ's footstool example

Here's a neat example that avoids two of these common objections in one go. If you're selling a footstool, for example, you already know the two biggest hesitations before the customer opens their mouth: space and price, as we've established.

So you deal with both in one calm, confident sentence: 'The great thing about a footstool is they're terrific value as an extra seat, and they take up very little room.'

That's two objections pre-handled in one breath. No resistance. No pushback. No need to defend the product later.

The principle

All of these examples do the same thing in different ways. They answer the customer's questions before they feel the need to ask them. Handled well, objections never actually become objections. They simply dissolve.

These are the golden rules of avoiding objections:

1. Know the most common objection for the product or range.

   - Upholstery: size, access, durability
   - Beds: size, comfort, support
   - Accessories: space and price
   - Finance: affordability

2. Handle objections early, not at the end. Once the customer is looking for an exit, you're already reacting.

3. Pre-handle, don't over-explain. One calm sentence beats a long justification every time.

4. Use normal conversation, not 'sales language.' The best objection handling doesn't sound like objection handling at all.

5. Assume reassurance, not hesitation.
   Customers often follow the confidence you set.

Avoiding objections is simple: answer the questions before they're asked. Get this right, and many sales that would have stalled quietly move forward instead.

Handling objections

When objections do appear, what matters is how you respond. Old-style selling techniques tried to argue customers into agreement. Modern selling is calm, logical and human.

An objection isn't a rejection. It's usually a request for reassurance.

Objections are often just questions. One of the most important mindset shifts you can make is this: many objections aren't objections at all. They're simply vocalised thoughts. Questions the customer is thinking out loud:

'It's more than I planned to spend.'

'Twelve weeks feels too long.'

'I'll need to check with my partner.'

Very often, these aren't barriers. They're moments where the customer is processing the decision.

If you treat every question like a challenge, you tense up. Your tone changes. You start defending instead of helping. For a long time, I did exactly that. I'm naturally competitive, and I found myself battling customers over what were really just reasonable questions.

The moment you ask yourself, 'Is this actually an objection, or is it just a question?,' everything changes. You stay calmer. More relaxed. More human. And so does the customer.

Don't just acknowledge objections, welcome them. When objections do surface, the instinct for many salespeople is to push back. The best salespeople do the opposite. They welcome them with phrases like:

'Of course.'

'Absolutely.'

'You're right.'

'That's a fair point.'

'Great question.'

Said genuinely, these lines immediately lower tension. They tell the customer that you respect their thinking, that you're comfortable with their question, and that this isn't a problem.

Welcoming an objection removes its emotional charge. It stops being a hurdle and becomes part of a normal, constructive conversation. Welcoming objections shows confidence. And confidence creates reassurance.

The ART structure

To keep objection handling simple and consistent, we use a three-step structure, known as the ART structure:

Acknowledge

Respond

Transition

Handled properly, objections don't stop momentum. They guide it. Let's look at some examples of this in action.

Example 1: Handling price

CUSTOMER: 'It's more than I planned to spend.'

SALESPERSON: **Acknowledge:** 'Of course. I completely understand. It's an important purchase. **Respond:** You mentioned wanting something that would see you out. This one's handmade, hardwood throughout and the display model still looks new after two years. **Transition:** Let me show you how this compares with another option at a slightly lower price so you can feel the difference.'

You haven't argued about price. You've reconnected it to value and kept the conversation moving.

Example 2: Handling delivery time

CUSTOMER: 'Twelve weeks feels too long.'

SALESPERSON: **Acknowledge:** 'Absolutely. Once you've chosen, you want it straight away. **Respond:** It's handmade to your order, not picked from a warehouse. That level of quality takes time. **Transition:** Let's reserve it today so your build slot starts straight away.'

The delay is reframed as a consequence of quality, not a problem.

Example 3: Handling 'I need to check with my partner'

CUSTOMER: 'I'll need to check with my partner.'

SALESPERSON: **Acknowledge:** 'Of course. You'll both be living with it. **Respond:** What usually happens is they say, "You've seen it, you decide." It often falls back to you. **Transition:** What do you think they'll say when you show them? Let's give them a quick call or video while you're here.'

No pressure. No confrontation. Just forward movement.

The principle

Handling objections isn't about clever comebacks. It's about staying calm, welcoming the concern, reconnecting to what matters and then moving forward naturally. When customers feel heard and respected, objections often strengthen the sale rather than weaken it.

These are the golden rules of handling objections:

1. First decide: is this an objection or just a question? Treating questions like objections creates resistance.
2. Welcome objections, don't fight them. 'Of course' and 'Great question' calm the conversation instantly.
3. Always acknowledge before you respond. People relax when they feel understood.
4. Respond with relevance, not defence. Link back to what the customer said matters to them.
5. Always transition forward. Never answer an objection and stop. Give the conversation somewhere to go.
6. Stay calm. Objections are normal. A customer giving you an objection is still engaged.
7. Listen carefully and flush out every objection early. Let them finish. Then ask, 'Is there anything else at all on your mind?' You want all concerns on the table at once.
8. Pause. A moment of silence keeps the tone calm and shows confidence.

9. Acknowledge and validate. 'I understand what you're saying.' It drops their guard.
10. Ask a quick clarifying question if needed. 'Do you mind if I ask what's making you feel that way?'
11. Use a method – especially Feel–Felt–Found.
    a. Feel: 'I understand how you feel.'
    b. Felt: 'Others felt the same.'
    c. Found: 'What they found was…'
12. Offer a clear solution or perspective. Use guarantees, stories, facts or proof.
13. Check in. 'Does that help?' Confirm the objection is gone.
14. Move forward confidently. 'Let's take another look at the colours.' 'Let me show you the difference.' Momentum matters.

Once you've dealt with the objections properly – avoiding the predictable ones, handling the natural ones and overcoming the deeper ones – the conversation changes. The customer stops weighing up *whether* to buy and starts deciding *what* to buy. The whole process becomes lighter because the hesitation has gone. This is when you can help them refine their choice, compare options, confirm combinations and allow them to picture the item in their home with confidence. From here, moving into the final concluding stage of the sale becomes smooth and professional because the solution is clear, the customer is comfortable and the path forward is obvious.

TIPS, TOOLS, TECHNIQUES, TRY

Tips

- Learn the essentials first. Master the best-selling ranges and the everyday questions customers actually ask, then build out from there.
- Open them up before closing them down. Start wide, let them explore, then gradually narrow to the best fits as you learn what matters most.
- Treat FAQs as your foundation knowledge. Combinations, fabrics, lead times, guarantees and cushion fillings are what make you sound credible and reassuring fast.
- Remember the customer doesn't want the quarter-inch drill. They want the quarter-inch hole. Sell the outcome, not the information.
- Pride and passion sell. Customers rarely know your story, so don't be shy about sharing it. Heritage and reliability build trust.

Tools

- Customer FAQ list by range/manufacturer. A written set of the real questions customers ask, used to train and test product confidence.
- Product Champion PDF (QR resource). A structured form to research one manufacturer properly and present it back to the team.
- Feature, bridge, advantage, benefit table. A simple sentence-builder that turns product facts into persuasive, customer-specific language.

- Your company's USPs sheet. A team-completed table that converts your real strengths into feature, bridge and benefit statements ready for the shop floor.
- Swatch control system. One swatch book and one colour family at a time, so you keep choices simple, relevant and easy to process.

Techniques

- Answer FAQs as solutions, not facts. Link the answer back to what they said matters, so the information feels personal and useful.
- Use the bridge lines properly: 'which is good for you because...,' 'great for you because...,' 'fantastic for you because...,' 'perfect for you because...'
- Add advantage only when you're comparing: 'The advantage of this over that one is...,' 'Where this really stands out is...,' 'What makes this different is...'
- Avoid downloading. Instead of pulling out everything, ask one narrowing question first: 'What colour did you have in mind?,' then show only what's relevant.
- Wrap USPs in a story, not a list. A simple heritage line, an origin detail, or a 'people buy from us because...' story lands far harder than bullet points.

Try

- Pick one manufacturer this week. Build the real FAQ list, practise the answers with a colleague, then test the team at the end of the week.
- Run the Feature and Benefit Game in store. Pick a product, list twenty-five features, convert them into benefits, then build bridges that sound like real conversation.
- Do a 'no downloading' day. Every time you feel the urge to list options, stop and ask a narrowing

question first, then only show what matches the customer's precise needs.

- Create ten store USPs as a team, then practise saying them out loud until they sound natural, confident and non-apologetic.
- Story swap. Each salesperson brings one product story (Vispring, Harrison Spinks, Stressless or other suppliers that your company sells, or your own company story) and practises using it to justify value.

8
Habit 6: Conclude

Why haven't we called this chapter 'Closing'? It's a fair question, and it's probably what many people expect at this point in the book. 'Closing' is the word most salespeople are used to. Close the sale. Get the order. Win the deal. After all, 'The ability to close the deal is the single most important skill in selling,' says Brian Tracy: 'everything else leads up to that moment.'[19]

That's precisely why we haven't used it.

In this book, we use the word 'concluding' very deliberately. If we called this chapter 'Closing,' most people would automatically assume we're talking about one specific moment at the very end of the conversation: asking for the order. That narrow definition misses what actually makes great furniture salespeople successful.

When we talk about concluding, we don't mean a single question at the end of the sale. We mean a mindset and a habit that runs all the way through the sales process. Concluding is what you are doing throughout the conversation and across visits: narrowing choices, gaining agreement, removing doubt, making small decisions and moving the customer steadily up the buying scale. Every visit should be concluded properly, even if the customer isn't buying that day.

In other words, concluding means *always* concluding. Always moving the customer forward. Always finishing each interaction with more clarity, more confidence and fewer unanswered questions than when it started.

Asking for the order is something different. That's what most people traditionally call 'the close.' It's the moment where you invite the customer to commit and place the order, when the opportunity is there, and winning it on the day. That is the ideal outcome, but it isn't always the reality in furniture retail. It's important, and we'll cover it properly, but it's only one part of the process. Asking for the order works best when everything leading up to it has been concluded well. In fact, when concluding has been done properly, asking for the order feels inevitable, because the customer is already happy with every element and smaller decision.

Many considered purchases aren't made on a first visit. Ask almost any salesperson what their first-time visit conversion rate is and you'll hear figures somewhere between 25% and 50%. Beds tend to be higher, other furniture lower, but even then, a consistent 50% would be very strong.

That's why concluding matters so much.

Even when you know a customer isn't going to buy on the first visit, you still keep a closing mentality. Not in desperation, but in determination: 'I'm still going to do everything I can with this browser or enquirer, because that will lead to a sale in the end.'

You may already know they're not a ten on the buying scale today, but your job is to find out where they are and move them further on.

That is what concluding really means: taking every customer as far up the buying journey as you possibly can, every single time.

Conclude well with everyone, on every visit, and closing stops being something you push for. It becomes something that happens naturally when the customer is ready.

A practical example of concluding across visits

It's a wet Wednesday afternoon. Footfall has been light all day when a woman comes into the store on her own. She's clear from the outset: 'I'm just browsing. I'm looking for ideas.' Less experienced salespeople might back off at that point. A good one doesn't.

Instead, the salesperson engages fully and calmly, asking the same questions they would with any other customer. Before long, they uncover the project: she and her partner are remodelling their back room. It's early days. She isn't buying today. She's at the very start of the buying scale.

But she is thinking.

They walk the showroom together, not rushing, not pushing. Sofas. Flooring. Layout ideas. Colours. As the conversation develops, something becomes clear: there are lots of elements to consider, but the sofa is the anchor decision. Everything else will follow once that's right. So, they conclude that visit properly.

They narrow it down to two sofa styles that suit the room and lifestyle. They talk through size, access, fabric durability and budget. She chooses a preferred shape and colour direction. The customer asks the salesperson to send a couple of swatches out. Before she leaves, they book an appointment for ten days' time, at the weekend, when her partner can come in.

That first visit hasn't produced an order, but it has been concluded well. The customer leaves clearer, more confident and with a plan.

Ten days later, she returns with her partner, exactly as arranged. This time, they spend a couple of hours in store. They sit. They compare. They ask better questions now because the groundwork has already been done. Together, they finalise the sofa choice.

With that decision made, the conversation naturally moves on to flooring that will work with it. Samples are looked at. A measure is arranged. Again, they don't buy everything that day, but the visit is concluded properly. Next steps are agreed.

The flooring is measured. Information is gathered. Options are narrowed.

The following weekend, the couple return. This time, everything comes together. The sofa. The flooring. A complementary dining piece that completes the space. The figures are clear. The interest-free finance option makes the overall investment comfortable and manageable.

They conclude the entire order. No pressure. No tricks. Just steady, professional progress across visits. That is what concluding looks like in the real world.

The order didn't happen on day one, but the sale was being built from the very first conversation. Each visit moved the customer further up the buying scale. Each interaction reduced uncertainty and increased confidence. And when the moment came to ask for the order, it didn't feel forced.

It felt inevitable.

Chase one rabbit

There's an old Chinese proverb that sums this up perfectly: 'Man who chases two rabbits catches none.' In furniture retail, this shows up every single day.

If the salesperson in the previous example hadn't fully committed to that woman on her first visit, there would never have been a second or a third. The bigger order wouldn't have happened. The relationship wouldn't have formed. The sale would have quietly died the moment the salesperson decided, 'She's just browsing.'

This is where many salespeople go wrong. They pre-judge. They label someone a tyre-kicker. They decide who is 'worth their time.' They chase today's order instead of respecting the buying journey.

The true professional doesn't do that. They understand that considered purchases unfold over time. They know that consistency beats desperation. They see every meaningful conversation as part of a longer arc, not a wasted opportunity if it doesn't convert immediately.

That's what 'chasing one rabbit' really means. It means committing fully to the customer in front of you, instead of half-serving five people while mentally hunting for a quicker win elsewhere. It means being present, focused and invested, even when the sale isn't going to happen today.

I saw this lesson play out perfectly with a woman called Julie Williams.

Julie had worked as a receptionist at Toni & Guy, a high-end hairdresser, for eighteen years. That alone told me a lot. She was exceptional with customers, warm, professional, trusted and was a brilliant representative for a premium brand. People instantly felt comfortable with her.

By her own admission, though, she wasn't a natural salesperson. She wasn't an instinctive closer. She cared deeply about people and wanted to look after them properly.

So I used to say to her, half-jokingly but always with purpose: 'Julie, you just need to become a salesperson, not a social worker.' And then I'd add, 'Chase one rabbit. Chase one rabbit.'

What I meant was simple. Play to your strengths. Be brilliant with customers. Stay with them. Don't abandon the relationship just because the order hasn't landed yet.

One weekend, I was working in the store Julie was in. On the Saturday, she had five outstanding conversations. Proper conversations. Time spent. Teas and coffees. Genuine rapport. Customers loved her. But by the end of the day, she hadn't written a single order.

When the store closed at six o'clock, she was in tears. I asked her what was wrong, and she replied that she had done no business and was disappointed with herself.

I told her the truth: 'Please don't be. I've watched you all day. You've spent time with people. They trust you. They like you. I don't have a single doubt that the hours you've invested today will come back to you.'

And they did.

The store opened at 11 am on Sunday morning. By 1 pm, four of those five customers had returned and placed their orders.

Julie hadn't chased five rabbits. She'd chased one, properly, five times.

She was the perfect example of relationship selling done right. Not pushy. Not desperate. Not distracted. Just present, professional and consistent.

That's what 'chase one rabbit' means. Commit to the customer in front of you. Respect the buying journey. Trust that time well spent compounds. When you do that, sales stop feeling forced, and more often than not, they come back to you.

Earning the right to ask for the order: The biggest mistake in sales

Many salespeople tell us they struggle, feel awkward, or even 'cheeky' when asking for the sale. One of the best ways to build your confidence is to ask yourself a fundamental question: Have I earned the right to ask for the order?

That means proving to yourself that you've:

- Built genuine rapport and trust with the customer
- Asked strong, open questions to understand their room, home and lifestyle

- Matched the product's size, style and functionality to their needs
- Checked that comfort and quality expectations are satisfied
- Confirmed that the colour, fabric or finish fits their taste and how they will use it
- Ensured that delivery, access and timing can be met
- Discussed and agreed on suitable payment or finance options
- Handled any objections or hesitations calmly and clearly

If you can confidently tick all of these, you've earned the right to close.

But here's the reality, this is the most common problem in sales. Every single day, in every kind of business, salespeople do all the hard work: they build rapport, ask good questions, demonstrate solutions and even overcome objections. However, right at the point of decision, they back off.

Instead of confidently asking for the order, they say things like:

- 'I'll leave it with you.'
- 'Have a think about it.'

- 'Here's some information to take away.'
- 'I'll give you a quote,' which really means, 'Here's a no-obligation bit of paperwork to escape from the store with.'

And the opportunity slips through their fingers.

Often, the customer is giving clear buying signals, asking questions about delivery times, finance options, fabrics, colours or stock availability. Those aren't casual enquiries. They are signs that the customer is leaning forward, mentally picturing ownership. Yet many salespeople don't recognise these signals for what they are.

If a customer is asking you detailed questions, they almost certainly *want to buy one*. That's your cue to switch into closing mode. Not pressure. Not tricks. Just a natural step into confirming what's essential, ticking the boxes in your mind and theirs, and asking for the order with confidence.

This links directly to what we explored earlier, closing if you can on the first visit, or concluding correctly if you can't. In both cases, the discipline is the same:

- Keep confirming along the way.
- Listen for signals.

- Make sure their must-haves are being met.
- Build their certainty and yours together.

When you do this, asking for the order doesn't feel pushy or uncomfortable. It feels natural, the obvious next step in a conversation where everything necessary has already been addressed.

Closing is never about pressure. It's about ticking the customer's boxes and removing any doubt. The order gets processed naturally when the customer feels certain that everything important to them has been satisfied.

The Five Cs: Summary closing

Before we walk through the Five Cs themselves, it's important to understand what they are and why they work.

The Five Cs were originally picked up from a brilliant salesperson called Ali Mehmet. What makes the technique so effective is that it doesn't feel like a close at all. It feels natural, visual and reassuring for the customer, while giving the salesperson a clear structure to follow.

This is delivered physically as well as verbally.

Hold your hand out in front of you, palm up, fingers open. Your hand becomes a visible checklist. Each finger represents a key decision the customer needs to make before they can comfortably go ahead. As you move through the fingers together, you are psychologically ticking the boxes with them.

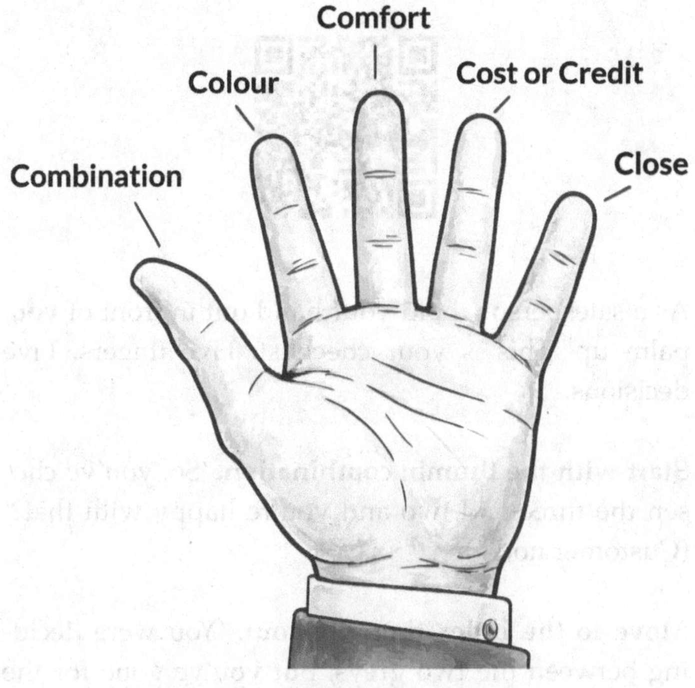

The Five Cs

People already do this unconsciously. Ask someone for their three must-haves and they'll often count them out on their fingers. The Five Cs simply turn that unconscious behaviour into a conscious reassurance process. You're proving to the customer that nothing has been missed. Everything has been covered. Every decision has been thought through.

This isn't pressure. It's clarity.

To watch a demonstration of the 5Cs close go to https://youtu.be/pG1YQK7uU9I or scan the QR code.

As a salesperson, hold your hand out in front of you, palm up. This is your checklist. Five fingers. Five decisions.

Start with the thumb: combination. 'So, you've chosen the three-and-two and you're happy with that?' (Customer nods.)

Move to the index finger: colour. 'You were deciding between the two greys, but you've gone for the mid-grey because it's light enough and practical. We're happy with that, yes?' (Customer agrees.)

Next, the middle finger: comfort. 'You wanted a higher back, some lumbar support and a seat that isn't too deep. So you're happy with that?' (Customer confirms.)

As you move through these first three, naturally weave in the customer's must-haves:

'You said it needed to sit below the windowsill, be practical for the kids and firm enough for your back. Are we happy those boxes are ticked?' (Customer agrees.)

Now move to the ring finger: cost or credit. 'While you're here, let me just run through your payment options.' Pause. Then deliver them calmly and clearly. Then stop talking. Smile. Hold the pause.

Very often, the customer will choose one of the options. When they do, the sale is effectively concluded right there.

By physically counting through thumb, index, middle and ring finger, you guide the customer through every decision in a clear, logical and reassuring way. Each 'yes' builds confidence. Each decision reduces doubt. By the end, the order doesn't feel forced. It feels like the obvious next step.

But what about the little finger? The final C? That's an important one, so we'll look at it in depth now.

'We need to think about it'

If you've been through the first four Cs and the customer doesn't choose a payment option, that's when we bring out the little finger: counter. (This one isn't for the customer; it's a reminder to you.)

For example, the customer may say something like, 'You've been great, but we never make a decision on the first visit, we need to think about it.' This is your cue. You're ready to respond calmly and professionally, rather than being caught off guard. What comes next is your counter, but because this one's so important, we'll cover it shortly in its own section.

We've all heard this hundreds of times, a phrase which usually means the customer is processing and needs reassurance. We usually get three reactions to this statement from salespeople.

One group think that this means the end of the sale. The other group have no idea how to handle it, and, worse, they actually accelerate the customer's exit by accepting this as a hard 'no' and immediately offer information or their business card in case the customer changes their mind. Finally, some salespeople even over-react emotionally to this objection. One highly experienced salesperson admitted that, when she heard it, she would snap her swatch book closed heavily on the desk. Another would literally slap his iPad down in frustration! These are all huge mistakes.

'We need to think about it' actually means, 'I'm almost there but there is some type of niggle or doubt that I need to remove before I feel comfortable enough to go ahead – please help me get there!' You see, 'We need to think about it' is *actually a buying signal.*

Here's how it often sounds in reality: 'You've been great. You're the first place we've been to, actually. So, if you can give us all the information, we want to go away and think about it.' At this moment, pressure has built up in the customer's mind. Their biggest fear is making the wrong decision. To protect themselves, they default to what feels safest: not going ahead. When this happens, your job is to release that pressure.

In that moment, the customer's mind is full of tension. Our job is to gently pop the balloon of pressure that's built up, not by pushing, but by reassuring. The way we do that is calmly, confidently and without rushing. Say, in a low, calm, relaxed tone, sitting back slightly with open palms: 'Of course, I understand,' and then pause before adding a simple question that has been responsible for millions of pounds of sales:

'If you don't mind me asking, what is it exactly that's causing you to hesitate?'

Then stop talking.

Let's look at that closely:

- 'Of course, I understand' shows empathy with their state of mind.
- Sitting back and opening your palms signals that you're relaxed, not defensive or desperate.

- 'If you don't mind me asking' gains permission and lowers the customer's defences.
- 'What is it exactly' sharpens their thinking and narrows it to specifics.
- '…that's causing you to hesitate?' presupposes they will buy, just not yet.
- And finally, silence. Let them fill it.

When you sit back and stay quiet, something powerful happens. The customer will often turn to their partner and say, 'Well… what is it exactly? What do you think, darling?' And the reply will come: 'Well, I like it if you like it.' Then the other says, 'So do I. Let's just go ahead.'

By giving them that quiet space, most people will sell it back to themselves. But never be afraid to genuinely find out what's behind their hesitation. That's all you're doing, calmly discovering what's holding them back.

If they still say, 'No, honestly, we never make a decision on the first visit,' that's fine. Circle back and go through the Five Cs again, super calm, super slow and using the same confirming language we've already covered. One finger at a time, calmly confirming what they've already agreed on. After each point: pause, look at both parties and let them discuss it in front of you.

- **Combination:** 'So, just for clarity, you were thinking of a corner group but you've decided that the classic three-and-two combination works better because of the layout of your room and the location of the doors, is that right?' (Pause. Look at them both. Let them talk.)
- **Colour:** 'And you were between several greys, but you've opted for the mid-grey because that's going to be the most practical with the children and the pets, is that right?' (Pause. Wait. Let them agree out loud.)
- **Comfort:** 'And the comfort; you said that was now more of a consideration, and you wanted support in the seat and the lumbar of the back region of the sofas, and this model, because of the ergonomic design, does that. Is that right?' (Pause again. Look at both. Let them confirm it to each other.)
- Here you can also reconfirm the must-haves: 'You needed the arms removable for access, a recliner built in and a fabric that can handle day-to-day use, that's all in place, yes?' (Pause. Wait for them to confirm.)
- **Cost or payment:** 'And you voiced an interest in the finance options early on. So, you've decided to opt for the interest-free option over a two-year period. You don't pay a penny in interest; it's exactly the same as paying cash, and your first payment isn't until a month after delivery. Are

you happy with that?' (Pause. Watch both of them. Let them nod or discuss in front of you.)

By slowly circling back and giving them space to agree, you allow the couple to nod, relax and realise that everything they wanted has been ticked off.

Very often at this point, they'll turn to each other and say: 'Do you know what, you're right. We're happy with it.' Because you've literally given them the space to think in front of you, the decision becomes clear and comfortable.

CASE STUDY: Terry's Story

Terry was a very experienced bed salesperson in his early sixties. A lovely, genuine man and highly knowledgeable. But he admitted that his biggest weakness was this moment. He didn't like to do what we've just described: circle back and ask the question. He felt it was 'pushing at the end.'

So, we gave him the words, the tone and the confidence: 'If you don't mind me asking, what exactly is causing you to hesitate?'

A couple of weeks later, just after a busy Easter promotion, we got an email from his manager, Brian. Terry had just wanted to say thanks. He converted four orders over Easter weekend by using that line. Three of the customers just discussed it in front of him. Another customer responded, 'We've always bought our beds from John Lewis, so we're going to have a look there.'

Terry calmly replied, 'Of course, absolutely no problem. Just to let you know, we have 109 models on display here, and I believe I've shown you the right one based on everything you told me. John Lewis only has fifty.'

The customer said they'd still go and have a look and walked towards the door. But when they reached the exit, they stopped for a few seconds, turned back around, and said: 'Do you know what? We're happy with it. We'll go for it.'

That one simple phrase, delivered calmly, gave Terry the confidence to ask the customer to give him the answer he needed and the opportunity to overcome that objection. He also gave the customer the space to think and discuss, right there in the store.

CASE STUDY: Neil's Story

Neil was a store manager we'd been working with. We drilled him relentlessly on his payment options until they flowed naturally. He practised them so often that, on the sales floor, he could deliver them without thinking.

One busy Easter weekend, Neil spent over an hour with an elderly couple who repeatedly said, 'We're not buying today.'

He didn't rush them. He invested the time. He got the comfort right, checked the fit, even showed them carpet samples to help them visualise the finished room.

Eventually, the customer asked, 'So how much is it?'

Neil replied, 'It's £4,200.'

The lady said, 'Oh my God, I'd better sit down.'

Because he was drilled and confident, Neil didn't panic. He didn't defend the price. He simply said: 'No problem, let me give you your payment options.'

And he went straight into his flow:

- Pay in full: £1,050 today, £3,150 before delivery.
- Or interest-free: £1,050 today, then £87.50 a month for thirty-six months.
- Or lowest monthly: £1,050 today, then £79.70 a month, starting a month after delivery.

The customer immediately chose the interest-free option and placed the order.

Neil later said: 'If I hadn't done that, they would have walked. £4,200 sounded more than they expected. They'd have said they needed to think about it. But because I gave them the options, they justified it to themselves: "It is £4,200, but I'm not paying it all at once. It's just £87.50 a month. That's manageable."'

Asking for the order

The single biggest mistake in furniture retail? Not asking.

Hospitalitynet states that 'the simple act of offering to secure the reservation made the caller 4.4 times more likely to book the reservation... Yet the study also found that hotel Guest Services Agents (GSR's) in the study only asked for the sale 52% of the time; call centers ask even less frequently at just 42%.'[20]

Closing isn't a trick. It's not pressure. It's service. Customers value clarity, reassurance and confidence at the moment of decision. A well-timed close removes doubt, gives them momentum and makes them feel good about moving forward.

Why salespeople don't ask for the order

If asking for the order is so important, why don't more salespeople do it? In our experience, the reasons usually fall into a few familiar categories:

- **Fear of rejection:** They've built rapport and don't want to risk hearing 'no.' Ironically, by not asking, they create a bigger risk as the customer is likely to leave without buying.
- **Lack of confidence:** They're not sure they've earned the right, or they doubt whether they've covered everything.
- **Not having the right words:** The best closers use the same close; one that suits them, their style, language and vocabulary.
- **Fear of being pushy:** They worry about coming across as aggressive. This is why we emphasise that closing is service, not pressure.

- **Ending on information, not action:** Many fall into the trap of giving a brochure or spec sheet and saying, 'I'll leave it with you.' It feels safe but abandons the customer at the moment they need clarity.
- **Misreading buying signals:** Customers ask about delivery dates, finance or fabric options, but the salesperson doesn't recognise these as signs the customer is ready.
- **Company culture or lack of training:** Some businesses don't encourage closing, or salespeople are never taught the skill. The emphasis is on product knowledge, not confidence at the close.

The bottom line: salespeople often don't ask for the order due to fear, habit or lack of confidence.

The closing toolbox

There's no one-size-fits-all phrase. Great salespeople carry a closing toolbox to suit different situations. The best don't rely on one magic line; they adapt their close to the customer and the moment.

Here are fifty proven closes that can be used in many different situations. Practise them. Use them. Rotate them until they feel natural. The key is always to ask, but to do it in a way that feels right for the conversation.

Direct closes:

1. 'Shall I get that ordered for you?'
2. 'Shall we go ahead and secure this while it's still in stock?'
3. 'All that's left is to get the order sorted. Shall we do that?'
4. 'Shall I put this through now while everything's fresh?'
5. 'I'll just take your postcode and we'll get started.'
6. 'Let's not lose momentum, shall I sort this for you?'
7. 'Happy to go ahead?'
8. 'Shall we lock this in?'
9. 'Would you like me to get this booked in for you?'
10. 'We're ready, shall we finalise the order?'
11. 'How would you like to pay?' (Then stay silent.)
12. 'Are we happy?'

Alternative closes:

13. 'Would you prefer to pay in full today or just leave a deposit?'

14. 'Would you like delivery this week or next?'
15. 'Would you prefer to collect or have it delivered?'
16. 'We're in your area next Wednesday or Friday, which suits you best?'
17. 'Do you want the standard layout or the corner configuration?'
18. 'Would you prefer leather or fabric on that model?'
19. 'Would you like matching cushions included or just the sofa?'
20. 'Do you want to take it today or have us hold it until you decide?'
21. 'Would you rather leave a deposit now or pay in full?'
22. 'Card or cash today?'
23. 'Do you want to celebrate with delivery before Christmas, or shall we make it a New Year's treat?'

Summary closes:

24. 'So we've got the five-seat in mid-grey, removable arms, memory foam cushions, delivery next week, does that all sound right?'
25. 'To confirm: you're choosing the three-and-two in that fabric, with free delivery and interest-free payment. Shall I process that for you?'

26. 'So, grey fabric, side table, extra cushions and delivery Friday, happy to go ahead?'
27. 'You've picked the design you love and the comfort you asked for, shall we get this set up for you?'
28. 'Everything you wanted is in place, would you like me to reserve that now?'
29. 'That ticks every box you mentioned, shall we make it yours today?'
30. 'We've got the right style, the right comfort and the right price, shall we go for it?'

Assumptive closes:

31. 'I'll schedule delivery for Tuesday.'
32. 'I'll get this assigned under your name, then confirm via email.'
33. 'I'll get the paperwork started, which card would you like to use?'
34. 'Let's get that order processed so it doesn't sell out.'
35. 'I'll book that in now so you don't lose it.'
36. 'Who's name shall we put the finance in?'

Leading closes:

37. 'Which room would this go in?'

38. 'What date would you like delivery?'
39. 'Shall I include the care plan while I'm at it?'
40. 'Shall I reserve that colour while I finalise the order?'
41. 'Let's check access for delivery, what's the best number to reach you on?'
42. 'What postcode should I arrange delivery to?'
43. 'How much deposit would you like to leave today?'
44. 'Would you like us to assemble it or deliver it in parts?'
45. 'Shall we pop a bow on it and call it yours?' (said with a smile)

Urgency/time-based closes:

46. 'We only have two left in that fabric, would you like me to reserve yours now?'
47. 'This price is only guaranteed till the end of the week, shall we lock it in?'
48. 'If we secure this today, we can still make your delivery slot next week.'
49. 'This model is being discontinued soon, would you like me to hold it for you?'
50. 'If I reserve it now, you won't miss out, shall I do that for you?'

51. Here's Russ Platts' best closing line: 'What do you think?' He asks this after summarising all of the customer decisions. He consistently sold £2 million worth of furniture every year.

With these fifty closes, you can adapt to every situation. Some are short and smiley. Some are assumptive. Some are about choice. Others are about timing or urgency.

The key is variety, and the confidence to actually ask.

TIPS, TOOLS, TECHNIQUES, TRY

Tips:

- **Define your terms.** *Concluding* means moving the customer forward throughout the conversation and across visits. *Closing* is the moment you ask for the order and win it.
- **Treat browsers like future buyers.** Don't pre-judge 'just browsing' as a timewaster. Stay present, ask proper questions and conclude the visit with clarity, next steps and commitment.
- **Chase one rabbit.** Commit fully to the customer in front of you instead of half-serving five people while hunting for a quick win. Time well spent compounds.
- **Earn the right to ask.** If you've built rapport, asked properly, matched the solution, confirmed must-haves, handled objections and covered delivery and payment, asking for the order becomes service, not pressure.

- **When you hear 'We need to think about it,' relax.** It's usually a buying signal, not a rejection. The customer is asking you to help them remove a niggle, not to hand them a brochure and let them escape.

Tools:

- **The Buying Scale.** Use it to locate what number the customer is today, and to measure your own effort. The job is always to move them up the scale on every single visit.
- **The Five Cs hand checklist.** Palm up, finger by finger: Combination, Colour, Comfort, Cost/Credit, Counter. It's visual, reassuring and keeps you structured.
- **Payment options close.** A simple service tool: 'While you're here, let me just give you your payment options.' Then present the options and finish with 'Which of those suits you best?'
- **The 'Hesitation Question.'** 'Of course, I understand... If you don't mind me asking, what exactly is causing you to hesitate?' Then stop talking and let them answer.
- **Appointment booking as a conclusion tool.** Don't let a browser drift. Conclude the visit by agreeing the next step in the diary (return visit with partner, measure booked, samples sent).

Techniques:

- **Conclude across visits.** Use visit one for clarity and a plan, visit two for narrowing and decisions, visit three for finalising and finance, so the order lands naturally.
- **Circle back through the Five Cs when they hesitate.** Slow it down, confirm each agreed decision, pause and let them agree out loud.

- **Use silence as a pressure release and a thinking space.** Ask the question, then stop talking. Customers often resolve their own doubt when you give them room.
- **Alternative-option closing.** Don't ask 'Do you want to buy?' Ask the service question that makes them choose: 'Which of those suits you best?'
- **Reframe 'think about it' as 'help me.'** Assume it's a niggle, not a no and go looking for the specific hesitation instead of defending or backing off.

Try:

- **Wet Wednesday browser drill.** Next time someone says, 'We're just browsing,' commit fully and conclude the visit with: two narrowed options, a takeaway action (swatches), and a booked return appointment.
- **Chase one rabbit for a week.** Fully serve the customer you're with, don't worry about what colleagues are selling, and keep the standard high. Put the effort in and it will pay off.
- **Ten-second silence practice.** Roleplay the hesitation question with a colleague and practise staying silent for a full ten seconds after asking it.
- **Five Cs hand rehearsal.** Practise the palm-up, finger-by-finger flow until it feels conversational, not scripted. Aim for slow, calm, confident.
- **Payment options habit.** Every time a customer feels broadly decided, use the exact line: 'While you're here, let me just give you your payment options,' then deliver three options and end with 'Which of those suits you best?'

9
Habit 7: Referrals And Recommendations

How many showrooms do you have? The answer should come quickly. One. Two. Five. Fifty.

People naturally think of physical stores. Maybe, after a pause, someone adds the website. Occasionally, someone suggests room sets. Every time, the answer is the same: *wrong*. The room goes quiet. People look puzzled. Then someone hesitates and says, 'Do you mean… customers' homes?'

Exactly.

Every customer who has ever bought from you now has a showroom of yours in their living room, bed-room or dining space. If you've been trading a few years, you don't have dozens of showrooms. You have hundreds. If you've been around decades, you have thousands. And if you've been established for generations, you have tens of thousands.

That realisation changes everything. Because once you understand that your biggest showroom isn't your shop floor but the homes of people who already trust you, the question becomes simple: how well are you using them? That's what this chapter is about.

Customers themselves often say, 'My house is like a showroom.' In fact, they'll often go further:

- 'Oh, my house is like a showroom for you.'
- 'I should have shares in this company!'
- 'I ought to be on extra discount, half my house is from here.'

They love saying that their home is full of your store's products and merchandise, almost as if they've become unofficial brand ambassadors. And clearly, if their house is full of your products, it's not just them who notices. Their family, friends, neighbours and colleagues will sit on your sofas, eat at your dining tables, admire your beds and wardrobes, and they will talk about them.

Research on social networks shows that the average adult has around 150 active social contacts. Within a home, a single piece of furniture can easily be seen, used or talked about by dozens of different people in the first year of ownership – dinner guests at your dining table, children's friends climbing on the bunks, colleagues visiting for coffee, relatives staying overnight.

Here's the clincher: UK consumer research shows that the average sofa is sat on by as many as 100 different people in its first five years of ownership; not just the household, but extended family, friends, visitors and social groups. Beds, dining tables and chairs show similar patterns. That means every furniture purchase is a live showroom piece that naturally advertises your store far beyond the original buyer.

The real question is: are we making the most of that? In most cases, we're not.

So, we ask our delegates: 'Do you carry business cards?' Everyone nods. 'And what do you do with them?' The usual answer: stapled to the paperwork, folded up, and handed over with the line, 'If you have any problems, give us a shout.'

So, we ask: 'Hands up, who wants more problems?' Nobody does. 'Who wants more business?' Every hand goes up.

Here is the shift. The primary purpose of a business card is to generate more business, not to be buried in a drawer. The way to do that is simple: give every buying customer two cards, one for them, one for someone they know.

We call this planting seeds for money trees.

Business cards correctly planted are the seeds to money trees

To be crystal clear about the metaphor: you are the money tree, your skill, care and follow-up create the fruit. The seeds you plant with every buying customer are your business cards. Timing is crucial: you place those seeds in the customer's hands only after they have signed their invoice and after you've shaken their hand. Delivered well, they will pass them to friends, relatives, colleagues and neighbours. Those seeds sprout as warm, trusting introductions that come back to you as extra business.

Use this wording, exactly as said, and say it warmly: 'It's been lovely to look after you. I hope you've enjoyed the experience.' And when they will say, 'Oh yes, we've absolutely loved it,' you continue: 'Great, well here are a couple of cards for you. It would mean a great deal to me if you could recommend me to friends, relatives, colleagues, neighbours or anyone you think might be in the market for what we sell. Please recommend me personally, I'd love to look after them.'

The crucial distinction

The danger with many salespeople is that they hand out cards indiscriminately, like confetti, before the customer has even bought, and they think that's enough to 'mark' the customer as their own.

Our co-author, Russ Platts, recounts a story of the time he attended a store opening where a group of salespeople had been brought in for the event. He got talking to a customer mid-morning:

> 'Aren't you going to give us one of your cards?' she asked.
>
> He replied: 'No, why would I do that?'
>
> She said: 'Well, every other salesperson has.'

Clearly, the customer was making the point that they felt like they were being processed.

This is why we make a sharp distinction: the only people who should get business cards are customers who have bought from you. Everybody else, we might give them a quotation, or a compliment slip, but we always collect their information for follow-up.

But for referrals to work, and for your own business cards to carry value, you must make the distinction: business cards go only to buyers.

CASE STUDY: Kerry and Emma

One of the clearest demonstrations of this came from Kerry at Glasswells.

On a Saturday, Kerry served a lady who had driven for two hours to get to the store. They chose a freestanding wardrobe package worth around £2,400. Kerry completed the paperwork, handed her two business cards with the right words, and asked her manager to come over.

The manager thanked the customer warmly by name, adding weight to the experience.

The following Wednesday, another woman arrived, waving a business card.

'Is Kerry in, please?'

'Yes, that's me.'

'You served my friend on Saturday. Could you show me the same wardrobes?'

Within minutes, she'd placed an order for the identical set, but mirrored, because their two semidetached houses were mirror images.

One sale became two because a seed, a business card, was planted in the right hands.

But here's the cautionary side. Two years later, when we spoke to Kerry again, she laughed and said, 'I'd completely forgotten about that habit!' That's the danger. We know it works, we see it work, but without discipline, we slip back into shortcuts. The lesson is clear: referrals are too valuable to leave to chance. They must be built into the system.

A more recent example involved a fantastic saleslady called Emma. When we trained her, we said, 'You'll have an order within a month or two of using this technique.'

In fact, she had two orders in two weeks.

- The first was a customer who walked back in carrying her business card.
- The second was another customer who came in with a photograph of her card on their phone.

It proved the technique beyond doubt.

Birds of a feather

People tend to associate with others who are at the same life stage or in similar circumstances:

- Young mums in their thirties will have a circle of friends who are also young mums in their thirties. They meet for coffee after the school run and swap stories. One of them says, 'I was in a shop today and met a fabulous salesperson who really helped me with X, Y and Z. I've got one of their cards, actually.'
- Ladies who lunch on a Friday will talk about where they've been shopping and who looked after them.

- Couples who have just paid off their mortgage, people downsizing, upsizing or buying holiday homes, all tend to know and socialise with others in the same position.

The point is that when one of them has a great experience with you, they will recommend you personally. These will often be the easiest orders you'll ever take, because trust is already half established before the new customer even steps into your store.

Referrals, reviews and Joe Girard

Referrals aren't just nice stories. They're measurable.

Research shows that around 88% of people trust recommendations from friends and family more than any advert. McKinsey estimates that word of mouth influences between 20% and 50% of all purchases. Long-term studies also show that referred customers deliver 16% more lifetime value than non-referred ones.[21]

This is true on both sides of the Atlantic. In the UK, review platforms like Trustpilot are enormously powerful. Over 90% of UK consumers recognise Trustpilot, and independent testing has shown that ads featuring Trustpilot stars are up between seven and ten times more likely to be clicked than identical ads featuring other review badges.[22] Feefo, another UK platform, analysed millions of verified reviews and proved that visible ratings directly impact buying decisions.[23]

In the US, consumer trust follows the same pattern. Surveys show that around three-quarters of Americans read and trust online reviews before making a purchase.[24] Third-party platforms, such as Yelp, Google, the Better Business Bureau, Amazon reviews and G2, carry significant weight. In fact, the Federal Trade Commission recently cracked down on fake reviews with new laws and heavy fines, making genuine, verified reviews more trusted than ever.[25]

The lesson is simple: word of mouth and verified reviews are the most persuasive forces in modern retail. When you hand over two business cards, you're triggering the most trusted source of influence a buyer has: the recommendation of someone they know. And when you pair that with visible, verified online proof, you double the effect.

No chapter on referrals would be complete without mentioning Joe Girard. Recognised by Guinness as the world's greatest car salesman, Girard sold 13,001 cars between 1963 and 1978, including 1,425 in a single year.[26]

His philosophy was simple but profound: the Law of 250. He believed every customer knows at least 250 people, enough to fill a wedding or a funeral. Treat one person well, and you don't just sell to them; you open the door to their circle.

Girard's method was relentlessly consistent. Every single customer got thank-you notes. Every single one got a follow-up. Every single one got two business cards: one to keep, one to give away.

We often think of referrals as something random and lucky. Girard proved they can be engineered. And what worked in Detroit car dealerships fifty years ago works just as well in UK furniture showrooms today.

Earn the right to ask

Some salespeople hesitate to ask for referrals because they feel awkward, as if they're begging. They're not.

Think about it: you've just delighted the customer. You've listened, advised, guided and helped them choose the perfect product. You've made the process enjoyable. You've already put in the work. You have earned the right to ask for recommendations. It's not begging, it's the natural next step in a brilliant customer experience. A happy buyer is usually more than willing to recommend your name, but only if you prompt them.

Peak-end rule

Psychologists Daniel Kahneman and Barbara Fredrickson famously demonstrated that people don't judge an experience by its length, or by every detail, but by two key points: the peak (the most intense or positive moment) and the end (the way it concludes). This is known as the peak-end rule.[27]

In a retail setting, it means your customer won't necessarily remember every step of their shopping journey. They'll remember the thrill of choosing (the peak) and the final impression you leave (the end). If the ending is rushed, flat or transactional, it can undo much of the goodwill you've built. But if it's warm, thoughtful and memorable, it cements the entire experience in a positive light.

So, finish brilliantly. The sale is agreed, the customer has signed the order, and the paperwork is complete. At that point, when everything is consolidated and their commitment is clear, that's the right moment to hand over two business cards.

You could finish with a handshake, or even a hug. Some customers are so delighted, and some salespeople so exceptional, that the moment genuinely calls for it.

Then, with the order complete and the cards handed over, you move into the second part of the 'ending on a high': invite your manager or assistant manager to come over, thank the customer by name, and add weight to the moment.

Every customer should feel *special and important*. The 'Manager Thank' (or assistant manager if the manager is unavailable) adds authority, recognition and an extra layer of care. Customers leave knowing they've been treated as special, not just processed.

The Disney mat

During our training, we talk about something we call the Disney mat. It isn't a physical mat, but a moment. It's the space at the top of the stairs, the edge of the department, or the entrance or exit of the store, where the customer leaves you. And it matters more than most people realise. This is the point where the sale may be complete, but the experience isn't.

The Disney mat is about switching into showtime one last time. It's a conscious decision to leave the customer on a high, with warmth, energy and genuine connection. Just like the best experiences at Disney, every interaction is designed to transfer a positive feeling. It's about sprinkling a little bit of magic onto a moment that might otherwise be hurried through, with the customer feeling 'processed.'

When handled well, this moment cements how the customer feels about you, your store and their purchase. That feeling is what they carry into their home, their conversations and their recommendations.

This is what we call 'completing the circle.'

The journey usually begins at the front of the department or at the front door. It should end with the same level of care, attention and theatre.

Once the order has been placed, the manager or assistant manager comes over to personally thank the customer. Not in a rushed way, but genuinely:

'Thank you very much for choosing us. It really does mean a lot that you've trusted us to help furnish your home.'

Then the salesperson takes responsibility for the final handover. They walk the customer to the edge of the department, the top of the stairs, the lift, the front door or, where appropriate, all the way to their car. On a wet day, carrying a store-branded umbrella and walking the customer outside is an extraordinarily high level of service, and one they will never forget.

As you walk side by side, calmly and naturally, you ask one simple question: 'If you don't mind me asking, where are you off to next?'

That question keeps the warmth alive, maintains connection and often opens the door to further conversation, further help and real-world opportunities that we'll explore next.

This is the Disney mat done properly. Not forced. Not scripted. Just thoughtful, human, memorable service at exactly the moment it matters most.

Real examples: Hidden opportunities

The following are all genuine examples of additional sales won by our delegates by asking 'Where are you off to next?' A salesperson had just sold a bedding order. At the till, they asked the customer, 'Where are you off to next?'

'We're going to buy a bunk bed from [competitor],' the customer replied.

'We sell bunk beds, let me show you,' the salesperson responded.

They walked the customer around the corner, showed the range and closed the bunk bed sale on the spot.

On another occasion, a grandmother came in on a Saturday lunchtime and bought three single beds for her grandchildren. At the till, the salesperson asked where she was off to next. She said: 'I'm going to [high-end retailer] to buy a [well-known brand] bed.'

The salesperson responded, 'We sell those.'

The customer replied, 'Yes, but they'll do me a deal.'

The salesperson simply said, 'I'll look after you, let me show you.'

Without discounting a penny, they secured the order for the brand beds then and there.

Both orders were unlocked by one simple question: where are you off to next?

Moments like these remind us how many hidden opportunities are missed every day. Customers often don't associate your store with the full range you offer:

- They don't realise you sell rugs.
- They don't notice you have a carpet or flooring department.
- They may not think of you for beds, mattresses or branded products.
- They may assume you only sell what they can see in the immediate department.

By asking 'Where are you off to next?,' you surface opportunities that would otherwise walk straight out of the door to a competitor.

Never ask 'Did you get everything you were looking for?' It's a rhetorical question. Almost everyone says yes. And an hour later, they're back in another shop buying the things they didn't know they needed.

'Where are you off to next?' keeps the conversation open.

Years ago, I experienced this brilliantly in a small, old-fashioned tile shop. I went in to collect tiles I'd ordered. As I was leaving, the owner casually asked if I was fitting them myself or getting someone in. I said I was doing it myself. He followed with, 'Have you done it before?' I hadn't.

What followed wasn't selling. It was expertise.

He explained I'd need a specific adhesive because the tiles were porous. He asked whether I wanted contrast or matching grout, then added the correct dye. He told me I'd need a sealant, wider spacers because of the tile size, and a simple plastic tool to finish the grout neatly.

I bought every single one of those items from him. Not because I was sold to, but because he asked the right questions at the right moment. If he hadn't, I would have discovered those needs later and gone elsewhere, probably to a place with less knowledge and less care.

That's the opportunity the Disney mat creates.

When you stay switched on at the exit, you don't just leave the customer feeling great. You help them think ahead. You protect the sale. And very often, you create another one.

Completing the circle

Escorting a customer to the front of the store, or even to their car, isn't just a polite extra, it's the final flourish in completing the circle you began when you first greeted them.

Picture this: you've just finished helping a family choose a new dining set. The paperwork is done, the cards are handed over, the manager has thanked them, and you walk with them through the showroom, chatting about delivery dates. As you reach the entrance, another couple has just stepped in. They stop, clearly seeing you finish up with your customers, who are laughing, shaking your hand, and saying, 'Thanks so much, you've been brilliant.'

Those new browsers have just watched you delight a customer. Subconsciously, they've seen the end of a great story and thought, 'This is the person we want to deal with.'

Many salespeople report that new customers literally wait at the door and say, 'When you're free, could you help us?' Warm and ready before you've even said hello.

Completing the circle does the approach for you. Instead of wondering how to break the ice, you've already shown incoming shoppers what kind of experience they can expect.

There can be nothing less threatening to a new customer than seeing you thrill and delight an existing customer as you say goodbye to them. Because when they see the smiles, the handshakes, the warmth and the genuine thanks, they're going to want to deal with you.

That's how great salespeople attract business without even trying, through visibility, warmth and genuine connection.

CASE STUDY: Kevin's Story – The Disney Mat

Kevin, a fifty-year-old veteran with over thirty years of sales experience, loved the whole idea of completing the circle.

Working at a busy retail park, he developed his own version of the habit. He said that, at the end of every sale, he would walk the customer to the front of the store and finish the experience there. He called it 'the Disney mat,' the place where he ended his show. This is why we call it a showroom.

Kevin would shake hands, sometimes hug the customer, always finishing with warmth and showmanship. He made every ending feel like the final scene of a performance.

A few weeks after starting this habit, he gave us feedback:

'Nearly every time, as I was finishing off with one customer, another was waiting for me. They'd seen what I'd just done. They'd felt the aura. They wanted to deal with me.'

He realised he was creating almost a conveyor belt of opportunities. By doing a fabulous job in full view, sometimes walking customers out to their cars with umbrellas when it was raining, and sometimes meeting them at their cars with umbrellas, he was constantly visible to new customers arriving.

And more often than not, as one sale ended, the next one was queuing itself up. Customers would say things like: 'Excuse me, we've come in to see about...' and they wanted Kevin.

For him, this wasn't just about courtesy. He said it was an absolute game-changer. Completing the circle turned him into the most in-demand salesperson on the shop floor.

TIPS, TOOLS, TECHNIQUES, TRY

Tips:

- **You don't have one showroom, you have thousands.** Every customer's home is a live showroom, and referrals are simply you learning to use them properly.
- **Referrals aren't luck, they're engineered.** If you want consistent recommendations, build them into the system, not into your mood.
- **Your business card is not for 'problems,' it's for business.** Stop stapling it to paperwork like an insurance policy. Treat it like a seed.

- **You've earned the right to ask.** If you've delighted them, asking for a recommendation isn't begging. It's the natural next step in a brilliant experience.
- **Finish brilliantly because the ending sticks.** The end of the experience can undo or cement everything, so treat the final moments like they matter. They do.

Tools:

- **The 'Two-Card' system.** One card for them for their next project. One card for someone else they know who would love your products and service.
- **Seeds to money trees.** Visualise it exactly like that. You are the money tree. The cards are the seeds. The fruit is repeat business and referrals.
- **The Manager Thank.** Bring the manager or assistant manager over to thank the customer by name after the order is placed to add weight to the moment.
- **The Disney mat.** A deliberate 'showtime' moment at the top of the stairs, edge of department, entrance or exit where you leave the customer on a high.
- **The 'Where are you off to next?' question.** A non-threatening open question that keeps the conversation alive and surfaces hidden opportunities.

Techniques:

- **Ask for the referral only after the customer has bought.** Business cards go to buyers. Never hand them out like confetti to mark customers as yours.
- **Use the exact warm wording before you hand out the cards.** 'It's been lovely to look after you. I hope you've enjoyed the experience.' Then ask for the recommendation.

- **Complete the circle.** Walk them back to where the journey started (stairs, lift, door, car). The escort is part of the performance, not a rushed exit.
- **Make the exit moment visible.** The most non-threatening thing you can do with a new customer is deal with another one fabulously. Let incoming browsers witness it.
- **Turn expertise into additional sales at the exit.** Don't ask 'Did you get everything you were looking for?' Keep it open, then diagnose what they might not have thought about yet.

Try:

- **Give every buying customer two cards this week. No exceptions.** One for their next project, one for someone they know. Make it a non-negotiable habit.
- **Run the Disney mat on every sale for seven days.** Manager Thank, then walk them to the edge of the department or door, end on a high, complete the circle.
- **Ask 'Where are you off to next?' to ten customers.** Track what comes back. You'll quickly see how many extra sales are hiding in plain sight.
- **Stop stapling cards to paperwork immediately.** Replace it with the spoken referral ask and the two-card handover, delivered with pride and warmth.
- **Start a simple referral log.** When someone walks in with a card or a photo of one, write it down. Proof builds belief, and belief builds consistency.

10

The Manager As Coach

I have a photo at home of my two boys. The younger one is gently resting his fingers on his brother's elbow as they talk about something. That picture, for me, captures what real coaching is; it's guidance offered with care, closeness and respect. Coaching isn't authority; it's partnership. It's about trying to help someone improve, grow or see something in a slightly different way.

The most influential person in any furniture store is the sales manager (or they should be). Their presence and leadership set the tone. A sales manager doesn't simply run the store; they set the standard for everyone else to follow. They lead by example and demonstrate what good looks like. They create the pace, the energy, the fun and culture of sales obsession every single day.

Too many managers, however, still believe that management is something that happens in a back office. They retreat behind a desk, spending their time on admin, complaints and problems, convincing themselves this is the heart of the role. It becomes a routine: walk in, head straight to the office, and only emerge when something forces them out.

Of course, complaints and admin need attention. But time always expands to fill the space you give it. If you let admin dominate your day, it will, and your sales team is left to fend for itself. That might be fine if every salesperson in your team is already world-class, but in reality, they aren't.

Think of football. A manager doesn't watch from the office and stroll out after the final whistle. They are on the sidelines for every minute of the match, guiding, encouraging, adjusting and setting the tone. A sales floor is no different. It is alive and in constant motion all day.

Never underestimate the effect of your behaviour as a leader and coach. In my experience, a good coach can lift performance in a store by 20%. A bad one can drag it down by 20%. The swing, positively or negatively, is enormous.

One client of ours recently illustrated this perfectly. They brought in a new sales manager, a natural leader with a passion for selling. He wasn't from the furniture retail industry, but he was a genuine 'people person.' He gave clear direction, he offered constructive feedback and, above all, his team quickly recognised that he had their best interests at heart. Respect was earned almost instantly.

The timing was ideal. He arrived just as we were delivering training and transformational follow-up. We worked with him, using the Seven Habits (which we'll look at in a moment) and the results spoke for themselves: an average uplift of 22.5% over a ten-week period compared to the same ten weeks the year before.

Even the best performers in the world rely on coaches. Novak Djokovic, one of the greatest tennis players of all time, has five of them, each one focusing on a different part of his game. The very best people in any field are coachable. They want to be stretched, challenged and supported.

Vince Lombardi, one of the greatest American football coaches of all time, once said, 'Coaches who can outline plays on a blackboard are a dime a dozen. The ones who win get inside their players and motivate.'[28] That is precisely what great sales managers do. They don't just recite the theory or get bogged down in numbers. They step into the action, motivate their people and inspire belief.

So, ask yourself honestly: does your team see you as a coach, standing alongside them on the shop floor? Or do they see you as a manager hidden away in the office, absent when it matters most?

What good coaching looks like in action

It is late morning on a busy Saturday. Families are drifting between the displays. The store has a buzz about it. The manager is on the floor, watching her team. She notices one of her salespeople approach a couple. The line comes out automatically: 'Are you OK there? Just give us a shout if you need anything.'

The couple smile politely, nod and wander away. The moment is lost.

Ideally, this should not be happening on a Saturday morning. If we've done our work in our training properly, those lazy approaches have already been ironed out during the week in huddles and roleplays. By the weekend, better habits should already feel natural.

But coaching never really finishes. Even after something has been trained, reminders are still needed. Old habits creep back. That is why coaching live on the floor matters so much.

The manager doesn't scold. She knows the salesperson is capable. They just need a reset or a reminder.

She moves quietly alongside them and privately says, 'Try it this way. Look them in the eye, smile and say, "Good afternoon, how are you today?" Then, when they answer, follow up with, "What brings you in today?" Let's see what happens. You've got this.' They say this with a smile. The salesperson nods, nervous but willing. Minutes later, another couple come in. This time, they try the new approach.

'Good afternoon, how are you today?'

'Yeah, we're good, thanks.'

'What brings you in today?'

'Well, we've just moved into a new house, and we're looking for a sofa that will last.'

Now the conversation flows. They talk about colours, comfort and room size. The salesperson is engaged. The customers are opening up. A few feet away, the manager gives a thumbs-up and whispers, 'That's it, brilliant start.'

This is coaching on-the-elbow. It is live, in the moment, catching people doing things right and steering them towards better habits. It turns what could have been another missed opportunity into the beginning of a potential order.

One habit. One line. One change. The whole customer experience shifts.

One habit at a time

At the heart of our training promise is this: the Seven Habits are worth at least one extra order per salesperson every week. We know that opportunity is there as an absolute minimum. Often, though, most salespeople don't know which of their habits is costing them that order. Scarily, neither does the coach until they think about the various elements within selling and the weaknesses in the salesperson's game that, when developed, will win that one order.

When I first started selling, my biggest weakness was my attitude and mindset. My mood fluctuated with my results. If sales were slow, my attitude sank. I convinced myself that Tuesdays were always quiet, or that certain weather killed trade. The truth was that my mindset was killing my performance. That was the first habit I needed to change.

That's a healthy way to begin a coaching conversation. Sit down with someone and say: 'You're good at a lot of things. But if there were one area you could sharpen, and it meant you'd earn an extra order every week, which one of the Seven Habits would it be?'

The Evaluator, explained below, helps guide this process. Most salespeople, when they examine their habits closely, know where to start. The key is to keep it simple. Don't try to fix everything at once. Focus on one habit at a time. That's how performance grows.

Consider the salesperson who slumped behind a desk when the store went quiet. A manager stepped in and said, 'Come on, let's get some energy back out there. Reset the display, smile and engage with those customers. Your attitude will set their mood.' Within minutes, the atmosphere changed and browsers became buyers.

Another manager set a challenge to tackle poor approaches. Her quietest salesperson was told, 'Give me five confident greetings before lunch.' By the end of the day, the once-shy colleague had written two orders.

A new starter who stuck to listing features was prompted to ask one simple question: 'What's the project?' That unlocked a full-house refurnishing order.

A salesperson who always jumped in too soon was asked to pause for three seconds before responding. On the very next customer, that pause allowed the buyer to add: 'It's for my husband's bad back.' That single detail changed the recommendation and secured the order.

The same principle applies to selling the solution, concluding and referrals. Whether it's linking back a feature to something the customer said earlier, offering a simple choice to bring the sale to a close, or handing out two business cards at the end of a successful conversation, one small nudge at a time can transform a salesperson's game. One extra order per salesperson, every week.

The Seven Habits Evaluator

To make this process effective, managers need more than gut instinct. They need a tool that shines a light on the details of each habit. This tool is the Seven Habits Evaluator, designed by Russ Platts, our Head of Learning and Development.

The Seven Habits Evaluator is a practical coaching tool that breaks selling into seven clear areas, the core habits. It turns vague opinions and generalities into specific, coachable behaviours. Managers and salespeople complete it side by side, scoring each habit against observable skills. The aim isn't to produce a single 'grade,' but to spot the one habit currently costing an order each week so coaching can focus there first. Used well, it sets the rhythm for development: quick on-the-elbow nudges on the shop floor, a weekly ten- or fifteen-minute check-in to review one habit, and a deeper monthly conversation if needed. Because both parties score it, gaps between self-perception and observed behaviour become visible, making the coaching conversation honest, specific and constructive. Over time, the Evaluator creates a shared language, a running log of progress, and a simple way to celebrate small wins while keeping attention on the changes that will move results.

Sales results alone don't tell the whole story. A low performer might not be weak everywhere; they might just have one habit holding them back. Likewise, a high performer might be getting away with weaknesses in certain areas that will eventually catch up with them. The Evaluator takes each habit and breaks it into its moving parts.

Below is the outline of the Seven Habits, along with the detailed skills and behaviours that sit within each one.

Mindset:

- Focus, resilience, positive mindset
- Openness and coachability
- Pre-judging
- Maintaining a consistent attitude regardless of circumstance
- Understanding the buying scale
- Belief drives behaviour

Approach:

- Pre-approach readiness
- Minimising 'minor time' and maximising 'major time'
- Warm, confident, non-threatening first contact

- Effective welcome and small talk
- Avoiding pre-judging
- Showroom awareness and timing
- Handling 'we're just looking'
- Re-approaching (feature + benefit with 'just to let you know…')
- Eliminating 'Are you OK?' or 'Can I help you?'

Questions:

- Million-dollar question: 'What's the project?'
- Using FAQs effectively ('When does the sale end?')
- Eliminating terrible questions
- Range of question types: softening, open (who, what, where, when, how)
- Drawing the room (funnel)
- Identifying must-haves
- Nail-down and usage questions

Listening:

- Active listening (eye contact, nodding, etc)
- Paraphrasing and parrot-phrasing
- 'Seven Yeses' technique

- Mirroring
- Linking back: 'Do you remember when you said…'

Solution:

- Ironing out the creases
- Turning features into benefits
- Highlighting USPs and KPIs
- Linking back to customer needs
- Demonstrating product knowledge with conviction
- Using the features-bridge-benefits method
- Ensuring all must-haves are ticked

Conclude:

- Moving up the buying scale
- Earning the right to close
- Using the 5Cs
- Handling 'We need to think about it'
- Arming the customer if the sale can't be closed today
- Asking for the order in different ways (summary close, combination, colour, comfort, must-haves ticked)

Referrals and recommendations:

- Giving two business cards
- Making customers feel special and important
- Completing the circle, manager / assistant thanking the customer for the order
- Walking the customer to the door or department edge
- Asking, 'Where are you heading next?'
- Ensuring quotes are not offered too early (close the order if possible, first)
- Consolidating the quote: walk through it, iron out creases, apply 'Seven Yeses'
- Highlighting savings within the quotation and trial closing ('So it's only £X, all we need is £Y deposit, are you happy to go ahead now?')
- Agreeing on the time and method of follow-up on every quotation

Scoring framework

For each habit, both the salesperson and manager score performance side by side.

Habit	Personal score	Manager score
Mindset		
Approach		

Questions
Listening
Selling the solution
Conclude
Referrals and recommendations
Questions and follow-up

This framework, created by Russ Platts, serves as the foundation for honest and detailed coaching conversations. It breaks down vague opinions into specific, coachable insights and gives both the manager and the salesperson a shared focus for improvement. To watch an explanatory video from Russ Platts about the best use of the Seven Habits Evaluator go to https://docs.google.com/spreadsheets/d/1Lah9AfwND1EKPRADbwwLvf48WBsNSuLi/edit?usp=sharing&ouid=107826597265984449606&rtpof=true&sd=true or scan the QR code.

Coaching on-the-elbow: Live examples

The most effective coaching is the kind that happens in the moment. A quick word at the right time or a nudge in the middle of a conversation can transform both the salesperson's confidence and the customer's experience, and win an order there and then.

A manager might remind someone that their energy sets the tone, prompting them to reset themselves with a smile. Moments later, a browsing couple stops, engages and buys. Another might encourage a colleague to drop the lazy 'Are you OK there?' and replace it with, 'Good afternoon, how are you today? What brings you in?' Immediately, conversations begin and orders follow.

Sometimes, it's a single question, like the million-dollar prompt – 'What's the project?' – that opens up an entire home refurnishing order. Sometimes, it's the discipline of waiting three seconds before replying that allows the customer to add a vital detail. Linking back features to a need the customer has expressed turns information into meaning. Offering a choice between grey and beige turns hesitation into a sale. Handing over two business cards creates the next lead.

These nudges are brief and ongoing, yet they have a profound effect. They don't feel like lectures; they are live on-the-elbow. They turn browsers into buyers, hesitation into orders and satisfied customers into future referrals. They are ongoing throughout the day as the sales manager-coach circles the floor, listens in, observes, catches people doing it right, praises, encourages, gets involved, gives the salesperson a suggestion, and is a positive influence on all of their interactions, being there as a quiet, helpful support provider. That adds huge value to both every member of the sales team and to customers.

Conversations that build trust

None of this works without trust. Stephen Covey called it *The Speed of Trust*: when trust is high, progress is fast; when it is low, everything slows down.[29] John Maxwell put it another way in *The 21 Irrefutable Laws of Leadership*: 'People buy into the leader before they buy into the vision.'[30] The same is true on the sales floor. Your team will buy into you before they buy into your coaching.

Trust is built in several ways. First, integrity. Conversations must be private, respectful and constructive. Criticising one team member in front of another destroys trust instantly.

Second, personal care. Get to know your people as people. What motivates them? What frustrates them? What are their ambitions? Show them that you have their best interests at heart.

TONE AND RESPECT: The Difference Between Telling And Coaching

I learned one of my biggest lessons as a manager early on. I was full of enthusiasm, passionate about selling and desperate to help my team succeed. But my tone let me down. I didn't realise it at the time, but what I thought was clear direction often came across as condescending or overly firm. I was *talking at* people, not *talking with* them.

It wasn't that I didn't care; I did, deeply. I wanted every member of my team to win, but my delivery created distance. The more I told, the less they listened. There was respect for my knowledge, perhaps, but not for my leadership.

The turning point came when I started to lower my tone, literally and figuratively. Instead of saying, 'You need to do it this way,' I began using phrases like, 'Let's work on this together,' or 'Try this and see how it feels,' The difference was instant. Barriers came down, conversations opened up and trust began to grow.

You see this kind of relationship all the time in sport. On the training ground, great managers don't bark orders, they smile, laugh, gesture and keep a hand on a player's shoulder as they guide, show and encourage. Their work is done at a calm, human level: *we're working on your game together.* That tone builds respect and belief far faster than any shouted command.

That doesn't mean all coaching should be soft or overly gentle. There are moments when a stronger hand is needed, when someone's been reminded ten times, or when a bad habit has become too costly to ignore. Just as in a match, there are times when you have to raise your voice, set clear expectations and demand better. But the difference is, if you've already built a relationship grounded in mutual respect and genuine care, those tougher moments land as guidance, not criticism.

The foundation of a great coaching relationship is trust, the trust from the coachee that you have their best interests at heart. That you have absolute integrity. That you are consistent. That you are there for them. That you give good feedback. And that you are absolutely dependable. The spirit of the relationship is simple: *we're in it together.*

Tone plays a huge part in that spirit. I developed a simple acronym that helped me to stay conscious of this whenever I was talking to one of my team: RAPT, as in *rapt attention*, which means to be fully present and deeply engaged with someone. It stands for Respect, Appreciation, Praise and Together:

- Respect for the person and their individuality
- Appreciation for their contribution and effort
- Praise that is specific and sincere
- Together, a constant reminder that we are working side by side

By quietly running that acronym through my mind before or during any conversation, I gradually trained myself to project that spirit. Slowly but surely, my relationships with my team improved, and over time, I became a much better and more effective coach.

After integrity and personal care, the third way to build trust is credibility. Demonstrate that what you are teaching is effective. Step onto the floor and demonstrate how to approach a customer, ask the right question or close with confidence. When your team sees it in action, your words carry more weight. A sales manager will often have been a really good salesperson, but we have to be careful because if you don't use it, you lose it. And certainly, if you're a sales manager and you're going to ask somebody to do something in a certain way, for example, meeting the approach with 'What brings you in today?,' you don't want to demonstrate the bad habit of 'Are you OK there?' You've got to have the integrity and credibility to do exactly what you're asking other people to do. Sometimes, the demonstration itself is enough, you don't need to say anything afterwards. Once they've seen you do it, the theory you've been talking about becomes evidence. It's an example for them to live up to.

Finally, there's consistency. Trust doesn't come from one good conversation. It builds over many moments, repeated with integrity, until the bank account of trust is full.

When trust is strong, coaching advice is not only heard but acted upon. Salespeople carry it onto the floor with energy and belief. With trust, even the smallest nudge creates transformation.

Energy, atmosphere and fun

Coaching should not feel burdensome. The best coaching brings energy, atmosphere and even fun to the floor.

Imagine two stores. In one, the atmosphere is flat. The team drift between customers, the music is dull and the manager is nowhere to be seen. Sales are written, but they are joyless. Mistakes are made, but no one learns from them. Customers sense the lack of energy and leave without buying.

Now picture another. The manager steps onto the floor with a spark of energy. 'Team, today's challenge is who can use the million-dollar question five times before lunch?' Smiles break out. A ripple of competition starts. By mid-morning, everyone is thinking about how to weave that question into conversations.

Throughout the day, the manager looks for small wins to celebrate. A salesperson paraphrases a customer beautifully, and the manager praises it with genuine appreciation. Another closes confidently, and a ripple of energy spreads to other salespeople. These moments cost nothing but they create momentum.

On the wall inside the office, a simple scoreboard tracks not only sales but also habits. Points for referrals, points for confident approaches, points for add-ons. It turns best practice into a game, and the more people buy in, the more enjoyable it becomes.

Customers sense the buzz. They are drawn in. Salespeople feel the lift. They look forward to being coached because it comes wrapped in encouragement, recognition and positivity.

Fun doesn't mean messing about. It means creating energy and lightness on the floor. It means smiles, laughter and the freedom for people to enjoy what they do. It's about passion and enthusiasm being visible, an atmosphere that lifts everyone's mood. Fun creates pride in the craft of selling and builds a store environment that both colleagues and customers genuinely want to be part of.

The Power Of Fun

One of the most overlooked parts of coaching is simply making selling fun. We are not in life-and-death territory here; we're selling furniture. Yet when pressure is applied in the wrong way, it can feel suffocating. The truth is, when the atmosphere is light, playful and energised, performance soars.

At the end of one winter sale, a manager introduced what became known as the hedgehog game. She brought in a simple hedgehog cake, filled with cocktail sticks tipped in different colours and hidden inside. Every time a salesperson wrote an order, they got to pull out a stick and reveal a prize. Some were small –

five minutes extra on their break or a longer lunch, for example. Others were bigger – a coffee voucher, a box of chocolates, even a free lunch. The mystery of what lay inside the cake kept the team buzzing all day. Sales flowed, laughter filled the air and customers couldn't help but be drawn into the upbeat atmosphere.

This is healthy competition at its best: light-hearted, energising and rewarding. It creates a sense of shared purpose without the heaviness of pressure.

It's a reminder of the world-famous *FISH! Philosophy*, which is built on four simple principles: Play, Make Their Day, Be There, and Choose Your Attitude.[31] When teams embrace those ideas, the store comes alive. They play with energy, lift each other's spirits, give customers their full attention, and choose to show up positively every day.

Fun, when led well, is never frivolous. It transforms the atmosphere, turning work into something people enjoy rather than endure. It builds a culture where laughter and lightness coexist with professionalism and pride.

A store that celebrates small wins, plays games, and shares moments of joy is not only a happier place to work but also a better place to buy.

What coaching delivers

When managers coach in this way, visible, consistent and energising, the results ripple through the entire team.

New starters don't spend weeks drifting, copying bad habits. Instead, they are guided from day one: 'Try greeting them like this… now ask the million-dollar question.' Within days, they are confident. Within weeks, they are contributing. They learn faster, and they learn the right way.

Underperformers don't drift endlessly. They are given clear goals, encouragement and feedback. One manager asked an underperformer to attempt three closes every day. By the end of the week, that salesperson had written more orders than in the previous fortnight combined. Hesitation became momentum.

Steady, reliable salespeople, the backbone of the team, often get overlooked. But coaching lifts them, too. A focus on better listening or stronger referrals can transform their results. Small lifts across the backbone make a huge difference to totals.

Even top performers benefit. Left alone, they may plateau. With coaching, they can stretch further, becoming role models and sharing techniques in huddles. One top seller, coached to present features as benefits, lifted his average transaction value by 15% in a single month. His colleagues followed suit.

And the customers feel it. They are greeted warmly, listened to properly and guided with confidence. Buying becomes easy, enjoyable and natural.

If one salesperson loses just a single order each week, that is ten orders a week lost in a ten-person team, forty a month, hundreds a year. Coaching can turn that around. The impact is enormous. A coach doesn't just change behaviour; they change results, atmosphere and lives.

The rhythm of a great coach

Great coaching has rhythm. It is not random or occasional. It is steady, reliable and something the team can depend on.

On the floor, rhythm looks like a manager who lives by the mantra 'Ten till four on the floor.' It means exactly what it says: from 10am until 4pm, managers are not confined to the office. They are out on the floor with their teams, coaching, encouraging and leading in real time.

We recommend that all of our clients adopt this approach. All admin, paperwork, rotas, and back-office tasks should be scheduled before 10am or after 4pm. Barring genuine emergencies, nothing should interfere with those key trading hours. This discipline creates a consistent culture across the business: the customer always comes first.

If you can't manage this to begin with, start smaller, 11am to 3pm, or even 12pm to 3pm, and build up from there. The important thing is to set aside dedicated time when the manager is physically on the floor in a helpful, visible and engaged way. Not standing back, managing, checking or criticising, but becoming part of the sales floor.

Small micro-conversations happen: a quick 'Well done on that greeting,' a nudge to ask a better question, a word of encouragement after a close. These touches, delivered consistently, shape habits more effectively than any spreadsheet or end-of-day report ever will.

But rhythm extends beyond the floor. It includes weekly check-ins with each person, ten minutes, not about targets, but about habits. 'How's your attitude this week? Which questions worked best for you?' It includes monthly conversations over coffee, talking about development and confidence, not just numbers.

This is the difference between focusing only on the scoreboard, sales, ATV (Average Transaction Value), and conversion, and focusing on the inputs that drive them: attitude, approach, questioning, listening, selling and closing. *Work consistently on the inputs, and the outputs take care of themselves.*

A strong rhythm blends short conversations on the shop floor, daily huddles, weekly check-ins and monthly coffee chats. Instead of reactive performance management, chasing numbers and firefighting problems, coaching becomes proactive. Eighty per cent of the manager's time is spent encouraging, sharpening and supporting.

The effect is striking. Underperformance becomes the exception. Not because the team magically changes, but because the manager consistently does the right things with the right people. Rhythm and rigour transform the store. They lift the floor, stretch the ceiling and keep everyone moving forward.

The salesperson as the coachee

Coaching is a two-way street. A great coach can only be effective if the salesperson is open to being coached. The best athletes in the world all have coaches, not because they're weak, but because they're committed to staying sharp. They are open to feedback, willing to adjust and always working on improving their game. A professional salesperson should be no different.

There shouldn't be any arrogance about it. You might be absolutely fantastic at what you do, and in many cases, it's only the lightest touch reminder that's needed, but the key is to remain open. A professional salesperson should welcome the right type of feedback, because that's how they continue to grow.

When you have a great coach and an open-minded coachee, it's a beautiful thing to see. Both the person and the performance grow. Conversations flow naturally, insights are shared honestly and development feels like a partnership, not an evaluation.

Think of coaching as a process of constant polishing. You're already good, that's not in doubt, but it's the expectation that we're always working on some element of continuous improvement. Just like an athlete fine-tuning their performance, a salesperson's game gets better with every small refinement.

The difference between managing and coaching

It's important to recognise that you'll always wear two hats: manager and coach. Both roles matter, and both are part of running a successful store. There are moments in every day when you have to manage – checking rotas, handling performance issues, resolving problems or giving direct instructions. That's normal. Management keeps the wheels turning.

Coaching is different. Coaching is about helping someone *think*, *see*, and *decide* for themselves. It's about asking rather than telling. It moves the focus from 'I'm in charge' to 'I'm here to help you get better.' Great managers learn to balance both, knowing when to direct and when to guide.

The behaviour might look similar, you're still talking, guiding, supporting, but the *tone* and *intention* are different. A manager checks and corrects; a coach observes and asks. Managing focuses on *tasks*; coaching focuses on *people*. You'll always have a foot in both camps, but the real magic happens when you lean more often into coaching.

The key difference is that coaching lives in the questions. Instead of jumping in with advice or answers, great coaches pause and ask questions that help the other person reflect, understand and grow.

Here are ten simple but powerful coaching questions that every sales manager can use on the shop floor:

- How's it going today?
- What's working well for you at the moment?
- What do you think could make that even better?
- What do you know about those customers?
- What's the one thing you'd like to improve this week?
- What's getting in your way?
- If you tried something different next time, what might that be?
- What did you notice about your last customer interaction?
- How can I best support you with that?
- What's one thing you'll take from this conversation?

Coaching conversations don't need to be long or formal. A single well-timed question on the floor can unlock insight, confidence and performance. Remember, the manager gives answers; the coach helps people find them.

Our challenge to you as the sales leader

If you've made it this far in the book, you're already different. You're not just reading about selling; you're reading about *leading*. And leadership in retail today means something more than managing, it means coaching.

Our challenge to you is simple but powerful: become a great coach of the Seven Habits. Live and breathe this book. Bring these principles to life on your sales floor every single day. Be the kind of coach whose influence is felt long after the day is done.

The role of the sales manager is not to sit in the office chasing numbers. It's to be present, visible, coaching, encouraging and energising; to be the person who transforms an ordinary store into an extraordinary one.

The challenge is not an easy one. It demands presence, patience and belief. It means living with rhythm and consistency. It means turning theory into evidence, coaching every habit, one salesperson, one customer, one conversation at a time.

All the great coaches we've ever admired, Sir Alex Ferguson, John Wooden, Vince Lombardi, Phil Jackson, Jill Ellis and Sarina Wiegman, share one thing in common: they built people first, and the results followed. Their teams played with belief because their leaders coached with care, trust and high standards.

The same applies here. If you're in a leadership or management role, somewhere along the way, *someone* coached you. Maybe it was a parent, a teacher, a manager or a mentor who saw something in you before you saw it in yourself. Think about that for a moment. That's the power you hold now, to be that person for someone else.

Customers feel it. Salespeople love it. Underperformance becomes the exception. When you lead with purpose and coach with belief, the scoreboard takes care of itself.

So here's our challenge to you:

- Be present.
- Coach the inputs.
- Catch people doing it right.
- Build trust, energy and rhythm.

- Create a culture where coaching never stops.
- Lead your store like a team, not a hierarchy.
- Be the person your team wants to emulate, not escape from.
- Above all, live the Seven Habits.

Because when you coach with care, belief and consistency, you don't just lead a team, you build a legacy. You shape lives, lift standards and make the sales floor a place of pride and performance.

That is your challenge. That is your opportunity. That is what great sales leadership truly looks like.

TIPS, TOOLS, TECHNIQUES, TRY

For managers and coaches

Tips:

- **The most influential person in any furniture store is the sales manager.** Your presence and leadership set the tone, so be seen as a coach on the shop floor, not a manager hidden in the office.
- **Don't try to fix everything at once.** Focus on one habit at a time, because one habit, one line, one change can shift the whole customer experience.
- **Spend the majority of your time coaching the inputs rather than obsessing over outputs.** Work on attitude, approach, questioning, listening, solution, concluding and referrals, and the scoreboard looks after itself.

- **Coaching isn't authority, it's partnership.** Correction should land as guidance, not criticism, and tone matters just as much as the message.
- **Coaching should bring energy, atmosphere and fun to the floor.** Lightness and healthy competition lift standards, lift mood, and customers feel it.

Tools:

- **Ten till four on the floor.** Ringfence the key trading hours for visible, live coaching, and do your admin before 10am or after 4pm wherever possible.
- **The Seven Habits Evaluator.** Complete it side by side, score each habit against observable behaviours, and use the gaps between self-score and manager score to guide honest coaching.
- **A simple coaching log.** Record the nudges you've given and the habits you're sharpening so progress becomes visible over weeks and months.
- **A habit scoreboard alongside the sales board.** Make good behaviours visible and celebrated, not just outcomes.
- **The RAPT check before any coaching conversation.** Respect, Appreciation, Praise and Together, a quick mental reset that keeps the spirit right.

Techniques:

- **Coaching on-the-elbow.** Quiet, in-the-moment prompts on the floor, followed by immediate reinforcement when they try it and it works.
- **Demonstrate what 'good' looks like.** Step in and show the approach, the question, the pause or the close, because credibility multiplies the impact.
- **Ask coaching questions instead of telling.** Use simple prompts like 'What worked?' 'What would

you change next time?' and 'How can I best support you?' to create reflection, not resentment.

- **Use short huddles and roleplay to iron out lazy habits before the weekend.** So better habits feel natural when it's busy.
- **Blend encouragement with clear standards.** Challenge is healthy when it's built on trust, and consistency is what turns coaching into culture.

Try:

- **Today, replace one poor approach with the coached version.** 'Good afternoon, how are you today?' then 'What brings you in today?' and watch how quickly conversations open up.
- **Choose one habit for the week and coach it relentlessly.** One extra order per salesperson, every week starts with one sharpened habit.
- **Catch three different people doing it right and acknowledge it in the moment.** Specific praise makes the behaviour repeatable.
- **Shadow one salesperson for fifteen minutes, then give one thing they did well and one small habit to polish.** Keep it simple, honest and constructive.
- **Run a five-minute huddle before lunch, set a small challenge and make it fun.** A store that's energised and coached is a better place to work and a better place to buy.

Conclusion

This book is a toolkit, but ultimately, it's about people.

Because retail is about people. Always has been. Always will be.

It begins with customers, the lifeblood of every store, every brand, every community. Customers who want to be understood, not sold to. Who value honesty, trust and care over gimmicks or pressure. And it continues with the people who serve them, the sales professionals, the managers and the leaders who turn everyday interactions into memorable experiences.

The habits you've read about are not optional extras. They are the difference between ordinary and outstanding in modern retail. In a world where customers are better informed, where choice is everywhere and where expectations are higher than ever, skill and professionalism have never mattered more.

For salespeople, these habits are the foundation of confidence and consistency. They help you stand out, build trust and earn loyalty, one conversation at a time. One extra order a week isn't wishful thinking; it's what happens when you raise your standards and follow a process that works.

For managers, these habits are the rhythm of great coaching. They take you off the office chair and put you back where you belong, shoulder to shoulder with your team, shaping behaviours that lift performance, morale and pride. When managers coach the *inputs* – mindset, approach, questions, listening and concluding – the *outputs* take care of themselves.

For directors, these habits are the blueprint for a winning sales culture. They create alignment across stores, consistency across regions and consistency of behaviour from top to bottom. Teams that live these habits don't just perform better; they create an environment where excellence becomes the norm, not the exception.

For owners, these habits represent something even greater: preservation and progress. Many retailers are custodians of generations of reputation, family names known and trusted in their communities for warmth, quality and care. These habits honour that legacy. They don't replace tradition with technique; they strengthen it through professionalism. They turn great service into extraordinary experiences, ensuring that every customer leaves feeling valued, delighted and eager to return.

That is how word of mouth is built. That is how brands endure.

It's often said that *people are a company's greatest asset*. And that's true, but only when they're developed. In our industry, fewer than 5% of furniture retailers invest in structured, professional training. Yet the evidence is clear: people + performance = profit.

When you grow your people, you grow everything; confidence, sales, service and your business.

This book gives you the habits, the language and the structure to begin that journey. But principles alone don't change outcomes; practice does. Repetition does. Coaching does. That's why the best retailers don't leave development to chance, they embed it, sustain it and surround themselves with the right support to make it live in every store, every day.

The opportunity is right in front of you, to be the salesperson who stands out, the manager who transforms a team, the director who shapes a culture, and the owner who leaves a legacy.

The habits are here. The next move is yours.

Author's Note

Thank you for reading this book.

The five of us, Adam Hankinson, Denholme Hankinson, Ruben Hankinson, Russ Platts and Dave Naughton, have dedicated our working lives to one central belief: people + performance = profit.

When people grow, performance grows. When performance grows, businesses thrive.

What you've read here is the product of decades spent on sales floors, in coaching sessions and alongside managers, directors and owners at every level of the furniture industry. These aren't theories, they're habits that work, proven through real conversations, real customers and real results.

We've seen again and again how *one extra order per salesperson per week* changes everything:

- For the salesperson, a boost in confidence and earnings
- For the manager, a stronger, prouder team
- For the director, alignment and momentum
- For the owner, a business that flourishes

Our hope is simple: that you not only read these habits, but live them, every day, in every conversation. Because that's how culture is built, customers are delighted and reputations are strengthened for generations to come.

With thanks and every success.

Adam Hankinson

Denholme Hankinson

Ruben Hankinson

Russ Platts

Dave Naughton

Notes

1 J Clear, *Atomic Habits* (Random House Business, 2018)
2 J Clear, *Atomic Habits* (Random House Business, 2018)
3 J Clear, *Atomic Habits* (Random House Business, 2018)
4 S Dolcos, Y Hu, A Iordan, M Moore and F Dolcos, 'Optimism and the brain: trait optimism mediates the protective role of the orbitofrontal cortex gray matter volume against anxiety,' *Social Cognitive and Affective Neuroscience*, 11/2 (2016), 263–271
5 BL Fredrickson, 'The role of positive emotions in positive psychology: The broaden-and-build theory of positive emotions,' *American Psychologist*, 56/3 (2001), 218–226, https://doi.org/10.1037/0003-066X.56.3.218

6 M Robbins, *The 5 Second Rule: Transform your life, work, and confidence with everyday courage* (Mel Robbins Production Inc, 2017)

7 J Willis and A Todorov, 'First impressions: Making up your mind after a 100-ms exposure to a face,' *Psychological Science*, 17/7 (2006), 592–598, https://doi.org/10.1111/j.1467-9280.2006.01750.x

8 D Carnegie, *How to Win Friends and Influence People* (Simon & Schuster, 1936)

9 S Agyei, 'Successful people ask better questions, and as a result, they get better answers,' *Medium* (9 November 2015), https://medium.com/@steveagyeibeyondlifestyle/successful-people-ask-better-questions-and-as-a-result-they-get-better-answers-46a46ba9fc3b, accessed 13 December 2025

10 Note: heavy-domestic rating is decided by the Martindale Rub Test – 25,000 rubs or more – but never mention this to a customer; it can just confuse them.

11 Scrivens Hearing Care (2019) *Sound Insight Report 2019: The state of the nation's attitudes to hearing loss* (Scrivens Hearing & OnePoll, 2019), https://scrivens.com/soundinsight2019.pdf, accessed 13 December 2025

12 T Hughes, *SPIN Selling Techniques: Stop talking and start listening* (Huthwaite International, 2021), www.huthwaiteinternational.com/blog/spin-selling-stop-talking-start-listening, accessed 13 December 2025

13 T Londergan, *The 4 Key Listening Habits of Successful Salespeople* (Salesfuel, 24 May 2021), https://salesfuel.com/the-4-key-listening-habits-of-successful-salespeople, accessed 5 February 2026

14 R Ramsey and R Sohi, 'Listening to your customers: The impact of perceived salesperson listening behavior on relationship outcomes,' *Journal of Personal Selling & Sales Management*, 17/1 (1997), 1–14

15 D Carnegie, *How to Win Friends and Influence People* (Simon & Schuster, 1936)

16 CL Kleinke, 'Gaze and eye contact: A research review,' *Journal of Nonverbal Behavior*, 10/4 (1986), 221–236

17 C Voss and T Raz, *Never Split the Difference: Negotiating as if your life depended on it* (Harper Business, 2016)

18 E Langer, A Blank and Chanowitz B, 'The mindlessness of ostensibly thoughtful action: The role of "placebic" information in interpersonal interaction,' *Journal of Personality and Social Psychology*, 36/6 (1978), 635–642

19 E Smith, *31 New Close the Deal Quotes that Drive More Sales* (CloseTheDeal.com, 2025), www.closethedeal.com/31-new-close-the-deal-quotes-that-drive-more-sales, accessed 13 December 2025

20 D Kennedy, *Ask for the Sale to Increase Bookings by 440%* (Hospitalitynet, 1 April 2021), www.hospitalitynet.org/opinion/4057147.html, accessed 5 February 2026

21 J Focken, *Referral Marketing Statistics* (JumpMD, 2024), https://jumpmd.com/referral-marketing/, accessed 13 December 2025

22 London Research, *The Impact of Customer Star Ratings and Reviews on UK Buying Behaviour* (2024), https://cdn.trustpilot.net/businesssite/LR-Trustpilot-UK-The-Impact-of-Customer-Star-Ratings-and-Reviews.pdf, accessed 13 December 2025

23 Feefo, *The Consumer Benchmark* (2024), https://business.feefo.com/hubfs/2024_Content/The_Consumer_Benchmark_From_Transactional_to_Value.pdf, accessed 13 December 2025

24 D Ruby, *30 Latest Online Review Statistics 2025* (DemandSage, 2025), www.demandsage.com/online-review-statistics/, accessed 13 December 2025

25 Federal Trade Commission, *Federal Trade Commission Announces Final Rule Banning Fake Reviews and Testimonials* (2024), www.ftc.gov/news-events/news/press-releases/2024/08/federal-trade-commission-announces-final-rule-banning-fake-reviews-testimonials, accessed 13 December 2025

26 J Girard, *How to Sell Anything to Anybody* (Touchstone, 2006)

27 BL Frederickson and D Kahneman, 'Duration neglect in retrospective evaluations of affective episodes,' *Journal of Personality and Social Psychology*, 65/1 (1993), 45–55, https://

psycnet.apa.org/doiLanding?doi=10.1037%2F0022-3514.65.1.45
28 BrainyQuote, www.brainyquote.com/quotes/vince_lombardi_165416, accessed 13 December 2025
29 S Covey, *The Speed of Trust* (Simon & Schuster, 2008)
30 J Maxwell, *21 Irrefutable Laws of Leadership: Follow them and people will follow you* (HarperCollins Leadership, 2007)
31 S Lundin, H Paul and J Christensen, *Fish!: A remarkable way to boost morale and improve results* (Hodder Paperback, 2002)

Acknowledgements

This book is the result of a lifetime spent in the furnishings industry. For over forty-five years, I have had the privilege of working with thousands of salespeople, store managers and business owners across the UK and Ireland. Much of what is in this book did not begin as theory. It was learned on showroom floors, through real conversations with customers, and by observing professionals who quietly mastered their craft.

I want to acknowledge everyone I have had the pleasure of working with over the years. Many of you will recognise things in this book that you have heard me say in training rooms, on shop floors or during countless conversations about selling and serving customers properly. Your ideas, questions, feedback and willingness to test these principles in the real world helped shape the habits described in this book. You will know who you are, and this work owes a great deal to you.

A special mention must go to Peter Lee, who was an extraordinary influence on my career. His guidance, encouragement and belief in me shaped the way I approached leadership, management and training. Without his support, I would never have become the manager, leader and trainer I eventually grew into.

My thanks also go to our customers – the retailers who trusted us enough to invite us into their businesses, to open themselves up to honest feedback and to allow us to challenge the status quo. That takes courage and professionalism. We developed many of the insights in this book alongside you.

I would also like to thank Julie Brown and the team at Rethink Press for their guidance, patience and professionalism in helping bring this book to life.

To those who have worked alongside me in developing these ideas, particularly Dave Naughton and Russ Platts, thank you for your experience, support and shared passion for raising standards in our industry.

I would also like to thank our LinkedIn audience. What began as a handful of short videos sharing practical sales tips grew, through your encouragement and engagement, into a much bigger conversation about professionalism in our industry. In many ways, that encouragement helped turn those early ideas into the book you are now holding.

Finally, my deepest thanks go to my family. To Wendy, Denholme and Ruben, thank you for your patience, encouragement and belief over the years. Your support has meant more than you probably realise.

Everything in this book comes down to habits – the small things done well, consistently, over time. I hope these habits serve the next generation of salespeople as well as they have served those who helped shape them.

The Author

Adam Hankinson is the UK's leading authority on furniture retail sales performance and creator of the Seven Habits programme trusted by many of the country's top retailers. He leads Furniture Sales Solutions (FSS), a multi-award-winning sales training company in the furniture retail sector, transforming sales teams across the UK and Ireland. FSS has been voted by customers and delegates across the industry as best sales training provider.

www.furnituresalessolutions.com

www.linkedin.com/company/furnituresalessolutions

www.ingramcontent.com/pod-product-compliance
Lightning Source LLC
LaVergne TN
LVHW040921110826
845155LV00041B/717